D1738117

YACHTSMAN'S LEGAL GUIDE TO CO-OWNERSHIP

YACHTSMAN'S LEGAL GUIDE TO CO-OWNERSHIP

by

Dexter and Paula Odin

John de Graff, Inc.
1981

ISBN Number: 0-8286-0087-0

Library of Congress Card Number: 80-71020

John de Graff, Inc.
Clinton Corners, New York 12514

Printed in the United States of America

To the memory of
Don Stevens
and our shared ventures

Contents

Preface

Walk into almost any bookstore today, and you can come out with the promise of becoming a better seaman. The shelves droop with manuals on sailing technique, boat maintenance, navigation, marlinspike skills, marine photography, galley cooking, and just about every other aspect of yachting you can imagine.

But as many boat owners will tell you, one of the greatest challenges of owning a boat is simply that: *owning* it. With competing demands on their time and money, even the most knowledgeable of seamen may have trouble finding a way to make boat owning worth all the expense and energy that goes into it.

Except for the rare live-aboards and world voyagers, few people in the vast yachting fraternity can utilize their boats fully. For most of us, owning a boat means constantly shuffling obligations to family, work, and other activities in order to find a few hours here and there for relaxing on the water.

If you're among that majority, there's probably nothing

you can do at the moment about the press of your commitments. But if your boat is going to sit idle for much of the season, why not turn that idle time into ready cash to help support your yachting pleasures? You can do that by taking on one or more co-owners for your boat. If you don't own a boat—perhaps because of the expenses involved—think about a joint ownership arrangement with someone who does. Or simply start from zero by finding other boating enthusiasts and purchasing a boat together. With our suggestions for joint boat ownership, you can decrease the burden of individual ownership without decreasing your use or enjoyment at all.

If you have already done that, there's nothing to preclude your making an agreement now. And for joint owners who have already worked out an agreement, we trust that you will benefit from checking this one against yours. It may be that in some respects we can offer you the "better mousetrap."

As we discuss co-ownership, its advantages will become obvious. You've possibly considered them before now. What may be even more significant to you is the realization that the pitfalls of a mutual undertaking like this come not so much from the number of people involved as from their lack of complete understanding of the venture. To launch such a relationship with no more than a handshake and a vague notion of the working details of the arrangement is to invite sure disaster.

Vital to the success of co-ownership is the partners' complete prior knowledge and understanding of all facets of the arrangement. Therein lies the often overlooked benefit of a written agreement. It serves both as a skeletal structure for the relationship and as a guide for ensuring that the participants have reached a full understanding and a true accord on all points.

This book, although short on words, has been long in the making. More than five years of first-hand trial and error have gone into developing the contract between co-owners, which we call the agreement. A legal background and over ten years of jointly owning different boats with various types of partners have given us a perspective that we think can benefit you.

We ask the understanding of the many women who have discovered the satisfactions of being skipper. Not wanting to perform major surgery on the traditional language of the sea, we count you among the yachtsmen, boatmen, and seamen for whom this is written.

Since there is no precedent for this kind of yachting guide, we're confident of a need for it and the prospect of future editions. In other words, we hope this is not the *last* word. For this reason, we would like to hear from anyone who, in using the book, has come up with additional or alternative suggestions.

Part

1

1

Why It Will Work

If someone asked you, "Would you like to share your boat?" you would probably give a negative reply. Guarded at best, your answer might run the spectrum from the merely suspicious to the explosive.

Since we don't want to begin with negative responses, we are taking a reciprocal bearing and asking instead: "Wouldn't you like for someone else to pay half your boating expenses?" You might react more positively to the idea of reducing your expenses to one-half, one-third, or even one-fourth of their current level—without sacrificing any use or enjoyment of your boat. And if you knew that an arrangement to provide these benefits also included help with the annual fitting out and the perennial chores that go along with owning a yacht, we might even expect a bit of enthusiasm to creep into your reaction.

In the pages to follow, we shall introduce you to an arrangement that produces these and additional benefits by providing for joint ownership—but separate and independent use—of your boat.

Joint ownership is certainly more familiar to the commercial fleet than to the yachting community; but in neither circle is it novel. Many owners of pleasure boats have discovered the advantages of such arrangements by now. Unfortunately, many others have ignored the opportunity. The reason isn't entirely clear. With few exceptions, a yacht is used so infrequently that two (or sometimes three or four) owners could make the fullest use of the vessel allowed by their individual circumstances without interfering with each other to any noticeable extent.

Some may fear that a joint ownership arrangement is riskier than sole ownership, doomed to fail. But many of the failures in joint boat ownership have nothing to do with the number of owners. The would-be sailor who buys a boat and then loses his enthusiasm—or discovers that there is more to seamanship than the salesman said—is bound to fail, whether he goes through it alone or in company. If he is a sole owner, it costs him at least twice as much to fail as it would otherwise.

Owners involved in joint arrangements might tell you that every failure resulting from the nature of joint ownership is offset by at least one survival solely because of it. Shored up by the economic benefits, fired by the mutual enthusiasm and comradeship of good partners, those who would not have made it as sole owners continue to enjoy yachting. Considering the escalating costs of boating and the dwindling availability of leisure time and marina space, they find the relationship more rewarding each day.

They could also tell you that they find it puzzling that some people who wouldn't hesitate to join a cooperative, buy a condominium, trade in the stock market, or enter into all sorts of co-ownership arrangements on land would nevertheless be reluctant to buy a boat with someone else.

While any of these undertakings involve hazards, the added risk of joint ownership can be insured against by forethought and good planning in most instances. In our opinion, the economic benefits alone justify the risks.

Perhaps the only reason more boats are not jointly owned is the scarcity of legal advice available to the yachtsman. Admiralty lawyers are, for the most part, servants of maritime commerce, insurance companies, and commercial seamen. Outside the specialty, you can find very few attorneys familiar with admiralty law—and those few are not likely to be your family lawyer. If you asked the average lawyer for an opinion concerning joint ownership of a boat, his own uncertainties about the subject would probably dictate a shake of the head and a verdict of "too risky!" Without access to an admiralty lawyer to correct the notion, or without a guide such as this book, too many good opportunities are lost.

That should not be. There is no reason to reject co-ownership simply because you cannot find answers to your questions, because the property happens to be located on water instead of land, or because it is intended for pleasure rather than for commerce. If, in the world of commercial shipping, joint ownership were deemed to be too hazardous a venture, we would expect to find more court cases in which the parties have sought a termination of the relationship. On the contrary, there are few—so few that, as late as 1964, Supreme Court Justice Hugo Black wrote, " . . . the scarcity of reported cases [involving disgruntled co-owners seeking a forced division and sale of a vessel] . . . indicates that establishment of a national partition rule is not of major importance to the shipping world."

The same advantages enjoyed by the owners of a commercial fishing trawler are available to the owners of that just-for-fun yacht sporting the tuna tower and outriggers. Or a racing sloop, a simple daysailer, a small outboard, even a rowboat.

Altogether, we have owned six boats with some eight partners. In the beginning, when we teamed up with our first partner to adopt *Puff* (a recycled tub from a local Boy Scout camp), we had no choice between joint and single ownership. But our imaginations flared in inverse proportion to our pocketbook. We closed our eyes and dreamed of the boat to come, the one we would someday have all to ourselves.

Over the years, though, something entirely unexpected happened. Instead of working our way into sole ownership of that big dream of a boat, we became firm proselytes of "co-boating." Now we find it inconsistent that so many boating enthusiasts, dedicated to sharing the actual use and enjoyment of their boats, wouldn't want to share the burdens of her ownership as well. Most of us, fantasies notwithstanding, are simply not of the same mold as Joshua Slocum. Rounding the Horn or crossing the Atlantic in solitary bravery may make fine reading; but is it what you want for yourself? (Even if the answer is yes, is it possible?) Buying, operating, and maintaining a boat by yourself sometimes seems to require no less courage and persistence. Is that what you truly want?

Almost any happy boat owner can become an even happier co-owner. The benefits far outweigh both the disadvantages and the risks. Certainly, the relationship carries risks different from those incurred in single ownership. But on the other hand, many of the risks and liabilities are reduced proportionately with the number of owners, just as the expenses are. And, as we will show, there's more to it than the added ballast in the billfold at the end of the month.

2

More Than Money

Next time you're strolling through a busy marina on a good cruising day, count the boats still tied to the dock. Chances are you'll come up with a surprisingly high ratio of idle boats to empty slips. Restlessly bobbing and tugging at their moorings, they appear to be signaling their impatience to the truant skippers—who, meanwhile, would be only too glad to take advantage of the day. But with all their other obligations, they cannot manage to get to their boats any more often than every second or third weekend. Chafing under the yoke and scheming to get away, they only intensify their stress.

You may be one of those unlucky boat owners. What are you going to do? Keep on writing checks for slip rental and upkeep, all the while repressing nibbles of guilt? Or will you turn your disadvantage into a distinct advantage? You could enjoy your boat to the fullest extent that your schedule allows and save money at the same time. All you need to do is take on another owner or two for your boat. Why not?

The burden of initial purchase alone induces some people to consider a joint ownership arrangement. But add to that insult the injury of inflated price tags on marine supplies, ever-increasing insurance premiums, skyrocketing yard maintenance fees, and those ingeniously extended taxes and license fees. Here's where consideration may become compulsion. Remember the one-liner that says if you like standing in a cold shower while tearing up hundred-dollar bills you will just love yachting? To the boat owner, it's no joke.

Joint ownership isn't a joke either. It isn't a "good news–bad news" story, where you know the part about cutting your expenses is going to be totally wiped out by whatever comes next. Because after that good news is only more of the same. The prospect of a heavier wallet—at least one that doesn't float away with the flotsam of a splintered budget—is not the only attraction.

In addition to savings in purchase and maintenance costs, you can save on fitting out. Many people with boat owning experience end up with a garage or storage room full of unused gear ripe for donation: compasses, life jackets, boarding ladders, anchor lights, galleyware, ditty bags, foul weather gear, charts, inboards, outboards, and you name it. In a group of three or four, at least one of you should have something to contribute as a gift or loan, thus enabling you to launch the association in champagne style.

For many yachtsmen the division of work is just as compelling a reason to share. If you are like most people, you would much rather have a half-day work party than sweat all day or all weekend scraping the hull alone. Since mutual owners share responsibility for keeping the boat in Bristol fashion, that means not only company during layups, but working cruises, with one or two partners tending to minor repairs while another mans the helm. On days like that, you may not actually save any time; but you're certain to have more fun spending it.

As for those small, unscheduled maintenance needs, one

partner can usually slip away to tend to some minor matter when the other partner or partners are too busy. There is always some easily overlooked item in need of repair. The sooner found, the cheaper the repair (and also the greater your chances of finding the problem before it becomes serious).

Safety is yet another factor, a vital one. The more owners there are to poke and putter around your boat, the greater the likelihood of discovering a hazard somewhere on her. In our personal experience in associations we have found a greater insistence that a safety flaw be corrected immediately than might have been the case if each one of us alone were in jeopardy. Who knows our individual pet fears? One of us may dread, above all, a gasoline explosion. He will insist on having either a diesel to begin with or a sniffer for the engine. Another partner worries about drowning and sees to it that the life jackets are top quality and that no one forgets to hold periodic man-overboard drills. Eventually, in an association, each owner comes to see and anticipate more danger than he would be likely to appreciate were he the sole owner.

Another benefit is the specialized knowledge or skills that each additional owner can bring to a partnership. From cooking to star gazing, yachting calls for an amazing variety of talents, and practically every potential partner can claim some proficiency or knowledge that will eventually benefit an association. Most of our associates have blessed us with their expertise—some of which they never realized would be used in a boating situation. Often what one partner can't repair himself, another can—true comfort when the maintenance yard sharks are taking passing jabs at your purse. And simply having a partner who knows one or two places where he can get a special break in services, goods, or technical advice can be a godsend.

In our own partnerships, both past and present, not only have we pooled our talents, but we've taught one another a great deal, too. Had it not been for our associates, learning

9

some of the basics of motor mechanics, sail repair, galley cooking, carpentry, and celestial navigation would have been twice as difficult and not half as much fun.

Now, novices may laugh at the way some owners humanize their boats, often to the point of absurdity. More than once, a casual comment about the fog eyes painted on the prow of our homemade *caique* put us on the defensive. In one respect, though, boats do resemble people. Indeed, they are more like people than they are like automobiles, with which they are sometimes erroneously categorized. The more exercise they get, the longer they stay in shape. Conversely, the less they move around, the faster they deteriorate.

Any good skipper who can afford the time tries to give his boat's motor a little workout each day for the sake of better performance. He also knows that the longer she sits in port without the washing movement through the water, the sooner her bottom will need scraping and repainting. If you aren't in a position to take your boat out for her own good, it's better to find another owner or two than to leave the old girl harnessed to the dock collecting barnacles. In a partnership, one owner can usually take her out when the others cannot.

Practical, budget-conscious boat lovers cannot help but appreciate these strong advantages of joint ownership: sharing the burdens of purchase and maintenance, dividing the chores, maintaining that extra margin of safety, tapping the special skills of the partners, and keeping the boat in better condition through frequent use.

The possibility of being forced by circumstances into joint ownership at some future time may sound remote. But not so many years ago, the notion of car pools for commuters also sounded far-fetched. According to census figures, boating is one of the fastest-growing recreational sports in the country. But while boats seem to be breeding like guppies, fewer new marinas are opening each year. Since the majority of boat owners do not enjoy the luxury of their private docks, this will mean competition for berths—frustrating if not fierce. Boating partnerships could eliminate some of the competition for *your* berth.

We have saved for last the brightest gem in the co-boating treasure chest. Friendship. Although it isn't guaranteed in joint ownership, the conditions are right. We're talking about the special kind of lasting friendship that develops from a common interest and a mutual source of pride.

Pleasure boating is more than mere pleasure. At its best it can be unfettered joy; but, as everyone who has ever owned a boat knows, it also means fear, anxiety, hardship, headaches. Anyone who survives these things with you is bound to become an enduring friend. And partners who sometimes venture forth together share the rough spots in a way that skipper and guest never can. If we're fated to run aground or put her on a reef, we'll elect any day to have a partner, not a passenger, at our side.

Chapter

3

Choosing Your Partner

By now perhaps you believe that joint ownership can be brimming with benefits, not laden with liabilities—provided, that is, you find the right partner. (For the sake of informality, we occasionally refer to the owners as partners; but they are actually co-owners, an altogether different legal kettle of fish.)

Whether you want to take on just one other owner or several will depend on your particular circumstances. Perhaps the simplest way to determine the right number of owners for you is to figure the boat's idle time under your individual ownership. If you anticipate that your boat will stay at the dock every other weekend, you have room for one partner. If you can use it only a third or a fourth of the time, you could take in two or three other owners without any reduction in your use or any inconvenience except having to plan the schedule in advance.

If this is the first time you have given co-ownership serious consideration, a few words will be helpful in the matter of choosing an associate.

You may be planning to select one from among your friends—predicated on similarity of social and vocational background, financial status, or geographical location ("Egad, a house right on the Sound!"). Naturally, you are going to take these things into account. But in our opinion, they do not constitute the ultimate measure by which to sound the worth of a prospective partner. First of all, how about taking a long, hard look at the individual's attitude toward boating? Only after you are sure that his outlook is compatible with yours and commensurate with the demands of the sea should you explore the possibilities of a partnership.

Prior to looking for other owners, though, a good move would be to think about any future associate's welfare rather than to worry about making the right selection. Ask yourself whether *you* will make a fit partner. Your self-assessment may surprise you.

If you do not own a boat already, are you quite sure that you like boating enough to commit yourself to everything that boat owning entails? You owe it to yourself, as well as to any future partners, to know whether you have a truly sustaining interest in the sport. Do you have the seamanship abilities requisite for the safety of your crew, your passengers, and the boat? Be honest. If you have doubts, it would be wise to stay out of an ownership association for the time being. Don't buy anything larger than a rowboat.

That's right, a rowboat. The novitiate with a will to learn would be much better off with a rented or borrowed one. He should practice rowing until he learns to row with automatic ease, forward and backward, with both oars simultaneously. Next should come long sessions with a manual on sailing—even if the ultimate aim is to own a power boat. *The Glénan's Sailing Manual,* found in most bookstores, marine supply houses, and libraries, is one of the best for both beginning and advanced seamen.

And then, back to the water with a rented Sunfish, El Toro, or any simple sailing dinghy. When the beginner learns to sail the dinghy wherever and whenever he wants it to go, perhaps with the aid of lessons, he is ready to own a small auxiliary daysailer or outboard. Thereafter, it would be only a matter of adjusting to the particular characteristics of later and bigger boats, whether under power or sail. No longer a beginner, by that time he should have been exposed to enough unpleasant weather to know that even with the simplest craft, there are moments of fright, days of discomfort, and a hell of a lot of work. Undoubtedly, he also will have either abandoned the idea of owning a boat or committed himself to it wholeheartedly.

If there is any secret to successful co-boating, it is probably this: allow yourself to get caught up in the sport as a sort of leisure profession, then find someone else who feels the same way about it. There, beyond a doubt, is your ideal partner. Beware the patio sailor, the fellow who ventures out only in fair weather and light winds, whose idea of boating is to sit regally at the helm of his yacht as she slithers through a dead calm. The first blow sends him home for good, his enthusiasm spent. When that is gone, just try to get him to help with the work. Forget it!

Much better to find the man or woman who has been out in a few rough spots and doesn't mind going back; someone who takes pride in a knowledge of seamanship; who spends wintry nights with boating manuals; who has been chastised more than once for tying knots on the furniture for practice; whose neighbors think him daft for his sudden bursts out into the street on a cold, starry night, sextant in hand. There is your partner.

Since this joint ownership arrangement entails separate use, the success of the relationship does not depend on social compatibility or a high tolerance of personal idiosyncrasies. During each partner's assigned period of use, the boat is exclusively his. No one else has the right to step aboard without his invitation. Naturally, if you happen to like cruising or racing together, you are doubly fortunate. But if, on the other hand, one of you insists on anchoring at

15

four o'clock sharp for a proper spot of tea while the other would just as soon open his beer with his teeth and toss a few along the way, that's no problem. You can see your boat frequently and your associates but seldom, if that is what you want. The encounters become even more scarce if you elect to pay for boatyard maintenance rather than doing it yourselves.

The areas of possible friction are thus reduced to only a few, which—assuming money is no problem—involve leaving the boat either dirty, damaged, or in danger. No good seaman could let himself commit such sacrilege. He would never want it thought, much less said, that he walked away and left the bilges dirty, left the vessel improperly secured, or neglected some dangerous condition. He realizes the danger of clutter in a seaway and the necessity for things to be in their proper places so they can be found instantly when needed. He knows well the invidious facility of the sea to take advantage of the careless or the slothful. "If you give the strange gods of the sea a chance," prophesied the poet Hilaire Belloc, "they will take a hundred and drown you for their pleasure."

Stated, then, in the simplest terms: Good seamanship leads to good partnerships. When you come across an able, enthusiastic seaman who wants to share in the venture, you know that you have found the right partner.

Budgeting
Shortgage or Surplus?

Nothing so detracts from the enjoyment of a boat—and nothing so threatens a partnership—as inadequate funds to support the venture. Troubles usually begin long before the onset of an actual money shortage. Sometimes the demands on available money push the owner to the point where he is weary of the obligation or feels guilty for straining the family budget. From that moment on, enjoyment begins to give around the edges. What began in a spirit of adventure and rejuvenation soon becomes drudgery, even the minor outlays stinging like sea urchins underfoot.

Maybe we sound too pessimistic. Isn't the avoidance of tight financial situations one of the primary benefits of co-ownership? It should be. But even the best partnership can be threatened by an unrealistic budget.

You may be thinking of beginning a partnership with someone who already owns a boat or taking on another owner or two for the boat you already have. In that case, you will miss the excitement of scouting for a boat together. But you will be that much further ahead for knowing in the beginning what your expenses are going to be.

The partnership budget not only takes into account the purchase price, the cost of fuel, the normally expected repairs and replacement of parts, hauling, scraping, and painting; it also includes insurance, slip rental, and any extra outfitting needed to get the boat seaworthy at the beginning of the partnership. Don't forget to crank in an estimated rise in annual cost due to inflation.

Experts claim that boats similar in size and characteristics require about the same budget for operation and maintenance; so a few well-directed questions around the boating community in your area could be of help in figuring your budget.

You can approach the finances of joint ownership in one of several ways, from the Spartan to the outright cavalier. The most conservative method is to stick to a boat that you could afford to purchase, operate, and maintain alone if you had to. This lets you cut your costs in half, by two-thirds, or by three-fourths or more, depending on the number of partners you have. Tight-fisted owners using this formula have no problem when it comes to major unexpected repairs, because they usually have a reserve on hand.

But not very many would-be owners, we suspect, can resist the prospect of something bigger and better than they could afford to buy alone. They want to take advantage of the joint ownership arrangement while still protecting themselves against the unforeseen exigencies of boating. If this description fits you, you'd best look for a boat that you know you could at least afford to operate and maintain alone, in case of some mishap.

Throwing all caution to the winds, you may nevertheless want to look for a boat that you could afford neither to purchase nor to maintain alone. In this case, make a careful budget—and estimate on the high side. Somehow, in the optimism peculiar to our species, we all tend to underestimate expenses.

Joint ownership doesn't mandate a boat with any particular set of characteristics. You and your prospective partners should have little trouble deciding what suits your mutual purposes and your particular area, if one of you does not already have a boat. We therefore offer only two suggestions. For the sake of easy maintenance and quick resale should the association end or should you and your partners decide to get another boat, we suggest a fiberglass hull rather than a wooden one. Further, select a design that has proved popular for your area.

For reasons admittedly more psychological than practical, we personally prefer the slightly used boat to the new one. The rate of depreciation for a new boat is greater than that for a used one, and that rapid new-to-used transition bothers us considerably more than the gentle progression from the merely "used" to the "more used." This has nothing to do with either looks or performance. Furthermore, a slightly used boat is often loaded with still-good equipment and offered at a bargain price.

In any case, if, as we suggest, you are in the used boat market, be sure to have the boat surveyed before obligating yourselves to buy.

Chapter

5

Plotting the Course to Accord

Suppose that now you have found the right partner or partners and the right boat. It wouldn't do merely to push all of you off to sea together with no more than a salute and a *bon voyage*. You'd most likely end up in a Sargasso Sea of ambiguity and conflicting aims. So it's time to get out the chafing gear.

You can find a variety of ways to minimize wear on mooring lines—from the most ingeniously devised covering to the traditional craftsmanship called worming and parceling. And so it is with a group of boat owners. As long as human beings interact, there will be points of strain that, without some type of buffer, could wear thin all original good intentions. Our proposed chafing gear takes the form of an agreement: a carefully thought out, written document. We think an agreement of this kind is essential to a successful joint ownership undertaking.

Authors Nicholas Healy and David Sharpe preface their widely known book *Admiralty* (St. Paul, Minn.: West, 1974) by explaining man's universal quest to introduce certainty through custom and contract into the "highly uncertain environment" of the sea. As they explain it, "Ever since mankind began making money by carrying things from one place to another in vessels, the shipping business has been characterized both by great uncertainty and profit or loss from a given voyage, and by an understandable insistence by investors, lenders, and shippers, that there be great certainty about everything that can be made certain."

The pleasure boat owner faces many of these same uncertainties. He, too, invests relatively large sums of money and time. But while a shipper's profits and losses are equated with hard cash, the yachtsman measures his profit in pleasure, pride, special friendships, memories, and other such intangibles. In both types of seagoing ventures, failures can occur for want of dealing with the uncertainties, insofar as they can be foreseen.

A contract such as the ownership agreement we will suggest does not indicate that the partners distrust each other. Rather, it is a way of eliminating uncertainties in the relationship and some of the uncertainties inherent in all boating. If you owned a boat alone, you would surely face many of the same vicissitudes that are bound to confront a group of co-owners. Ignore them if you wish, but they're lying in wait all the same.

Facing the uncertainties is one of the built-in pluses of a joint ownership agreement, in that it requires forethought, sound planning, and a proper assessment of the undertaking before it ever commences. So an important purpose of the agreement is accomplished before even one signature is affixed. If you don't take the time to consider each facet of the relationship with your future partner or partners, how can you presume that you truly agree on every detail? Where are you going to keep the boat? How do you divide its use? How are you going to care for it? What happens if death, disability, or some other tragedy should strike?

Perhaps you can see why the preparation and consideration of an agreement is fully as important as its existence in the form of a legal document. Those about to embark on a joint venture are required, much more than the sole boat owner, to consider the full measure of the undertaking. The agreement becomes a kind of sounding board by which the future partners can tell whether there is a common accord on all the points. And it further enables each party to see what decisions affecting him will be surrendered up to mutual consent.

For two or more of you to say that you will decide how to solve problems as they arise is to put too heavy a burden on yourselves. Sometimes it works. But why take that chance? Agree in advance, and you know that you have an understanding. To leave matters until they come up, and then hope for an accord, is a move that you wouldn't entertain in any serious undertaking (except, maybe, in matters of the heart, a subject unlike any other). Remember also that in at least two specific situations—the death or mental incapacity of one of you—the parties can agree on a course of action *only* in advance.

In dealing with a friend, you might hear someone say, "Come on, we're good friends! All we really need is a handshake." But that's missing the point. You owe it to each other, *especially* if you are good friends, to make sure that you are in complete agreement—even if you never do get around to signing the contract itself.

Perhaps a simpler way to make the point is to say that it's a mistake to think that a piece of paper bearing signatures and a notary's seal constitutes an agreement. Certainly it's a contract, enforceable by the courts. You are legally bound by it. But a true agreement, the harmony between minds, exists only when two or more people come to a complete understanding of something that is going to be mutually beneficial. To do this, each person must be as diligent in considering the other person's position as he is in studying his own.

Look at it in a business context. Suppose, for instance, that you are in business for yourself, and you need a certain component that your engineers have spent years designing. You know that it will cost at least $100 per component to make. You ask a manufacturer for a bid, and to your surprise he comes back with $75 for each unit. So you quickly agree to his terms. Do you have an agreement? You do have a contract, yes, but there is no actual agreement. The manufacturer obviously didn't understand what was involved, and he bid against his own self-interest. If you go ahead with the arrangement and he loses too much from it, one way or another he will break the contract—even if it's through bankruptcy. Result? Litigation, concomitant hard feelings, losses on both sides.

If you had wanted a true agreement, you would have made certain that he fully understood the undertaking by discussing with him the cost known to you. Then you would have had not only a contract, but a true accord. The by-product: a steady supply of the component you need, a manufacturer eager to join you in future enterprises, and maybe a business and friendship combination that will ultimately be your greatest reward.

Some business people question the need for such an accord. They seek only contracts, and of course many of them prosper through this approach. But even this type of person would probably agree that it would be fatal in a boating partnership.

So seek both the contract and the accord. If you doubt that you or one of your prospective partners can afford the expense without guilt or undue personal sacrifice, bring your doubts out into the open. When you see disadvantages for any of you in some part of the agreement, discuss your reservations. Then, if a mistake is made in some particular, it will be a mutual one.

Now let's move on from the agreement in spirit to the agreement on paper. Lawyers are great form users, generally maintaining files of forms for contracts, deeds, leases, wills, and all sorts of court pleadings. To be frank, what the legal profession often calls an original legal document or legal research is nothing more than a combination and modification of several forms to fit a particular situation.

Forms are used for several very good reasons. Drawing up a completely original document every time a contract is needed would be time-consuming, expensive, and—in many cases—altogether unnecessary. As time-savers in drafting contracts and pleadings, forms are of indisputable value. Lawyers also use them as a sort of checklist to be sure that they have covered all the relevant points of a contract.

The following chapter presents and discusses, clause by clause, a form agreement for joint boat ownership. You will find it useful both as a guide to mutual understanding and as a legal document, the structure that will form the basic design of your partnership. In most cases, the agreement should be reviewed by a lawyer in your area for any minor modifications needed to conform to local laws.

If your boat represents a very small investment to you— say, only a few hundred dollars—you may not want to go to the expense of consulting a lawyer (unless one happens to be a good friend or to live next door). But you should remember that claims for injuries that can arise from the use of a boat are seldom proportionate to the boat's value. While we're confident you'll be better off with the executed agreement than without it, you'll sleep more soundly if it has the sanction of competent counsel.

However, you may be among those many boat owners who invest considerably more in their pleasure (and whose boats are sometimes worth even more than their houses). You also should use the form to help you and your associates discover exactly what you want in the relationship. Then, after selecting the provisions that you need, with any changes you see fit, draw it up and take it to a lawyer. Legal modifications that your lawyer makes to conform to local laws may look slight, but they are important, since yachtsmen are subject not only to admiralty (federal) laws, but also to numerous constantly changing state laws. No one form will fit the peculiarities of every relationship or be precisely accurate for every jurisdiction. The fine tuning must be left to the local attorney.

In Chapter 6 every clause, or provision, of the agreement is followed by a discussion of its intent—the reason that it is necessary—and a consideration of any alternative provision you may want to use instead. The checklist in Chapter 7 can be used as a worksheet in conjunction with your study of the agreement. It will remind you of essential questions you should be asking yourselves about the many facets of your proposed association.

Except for professional review and minor changes, you will have done most of the lawyer's work for yourselves. More important, you will have accomplished the most significant and time-consuming part of a good legal draftsman's job: anticipating all the contingencies that may arise in a relationship and providing for them—insofar as humanly possible.

Imagine the time it would take if you were to sit down with your counsel and explore all the aspects of a contract not yet written or thought out. A lengthy, two-way process would have to take place: your telling him what you think you want, and his explaining to you, in turn, what such a contract would entail. After that drawn-out consultation would come hours of the lawyer's time in drafting—and even more hours if the lawyer weren't familiar with yachting. All this, of course, at your expense.

Although this form won't save you all the legal fees, it will assuredly cut them to a fraction of what you would otherwise incur. No lawyer who has the client's best interests at heart will object one whit to something that saves him time and saves his client money. In fact, if there is anything like a universal lawyer's prayer, it is that all clients know what they want before they walk in the door. Since very few forms of this kind of contract are in existence, most lawyers would welcome you, the form, and your state of preparedness as a rare combination in answer to that prayer.

The one thing you should not do is sign the agreement first and *then* take it to a lawyer. Attorneys have been known to tell their clients, tongue-in-cheek, to do just that, because their fees for any initial advising, review, or drafting of a good contract are peanuts compared to those they get for untangling a bad one.

It's quite true that you might have bought a car, a boat, even your home, with a form contract, never seeing a lawyer in the process. And you could use this agreement in the same way, as we've said you might want to do if the boat involved is worth less than the legal services would cost. But even then, we recommend a professional review, because the value of the boat isn't the only thing you have to consider. A forty-year-old bargain could eventually prove more costly than Cleopatra's barge if her unseaworthy condition resulted in third-party liabilities. Outboards costing less than a thousand dollars have been known to inflict million-dollar injuries. We include a fuller discussion of liability safeguards in the explanation of the uninsured claims clause.

To make the best use of this book, we suggest you give the following chapter (the agreement and explanation) a quick reading all the way through to get some idea of the scope of the agreement. After that, you can get down to the business of creating your own contract with a more thorough study of each clause, using the checklist in Chapter 7 as a prod to your memory.

Part
2

Chapter

6

Agreement
and Explanation

Purpose

1. With implicit trust in each other, a common appreciation
of the sea, and a desire to unite in the ownership of a
pleasure yacht, we enter into this Agreement to provide
a better understanding of our mutual expectations and a
greater awareness of our fiducial obligations to one
another.

Except for the business about a fiducial obligation, this
introductory clause, like so much of the agreement, carries
more practical than legal significance. It provides the parties with a checklist for the initial decision whether to form
the association or not.

Without mutual, implicit trust and an appreciation for
seamanship, water hazards, boating perils, and the pleasures
(and pleasurable discomforts) of the waterman's life, it's
better to pause and reconsider your desire to own a boat
together.

Now, what about that scary phrase, "fiducial obligations"? Ominous as the two words may sound, they are necessary to convey to all parties concerned, and to the world, the fact that you, the owners, are to perform the agreement as fiduciaries—trustees, if you will. Just as trustees and guardians are required to protect and act only in the best interests of children, the aged, or the ill, so are the owners required to act toward each other. A trusteeship requires the highest degree of integrity. If one of you seems unwilling or unable to fulfill this obligation, you had better stop in your wake and begin looking for someone else.

"To provide a better understanding" is the essence of the agreement: an expression of a true accord, not merely a collection of signatures on a piece of paper. As discussed earlier, this means sitting down with your prospective associates to consider each portion of the agreement. What will you do in case of some unforeseen financial hardship or the death or disability of one of you? If one partner suddenly has to move away from the area, what then? And how, exactly, are you going to handle the expenses? Scheduling? Chores? Who should be allowed to operate the boat? Many of these things don't seem important during the euphoria of early ownership. And some of them aren't fitting subjects for a relaxed evening chat. But asking yourselves the right questions at the start is what this book is all about. It's also a plan to foresee, come to grips with, and so disarm, any unplanned turn of events.

So don't just read through and execute this contract: *study it together*. Toss it around for discussion. Agree or disagree with each provision. Only to the extent that the contract helps create a good, sound relationship can it be beneficial to you.

Interpretation

2. As we understand our obligations, so are they to be construed by others, in accordance with the laws applicable within the [Commonwealth/State of

_____], and governed by that interpretation which best accomplishes these, our common objectives:

a. To indulge each other, but at no greater risk or sacrifice than is inherent in our joint dominion, so that to the fullest extent possible we may each enjoy the use and ownership of a safe and seaworthy yacht, operated strictly for our personal pleasure and kept at a cost neither greater nor less than that required to constantly maintain the vessel in a dependable and proudly presentable condition; and

b. To be ever aware of our duty to conserve funds, but never by risking our safety or sacrificing our pleasure, and to be always mindful that a few pennies yielded up to accommodate one of us is more than compensated for by the aggregate of our mutual contributions.

Since boats are portable, they are likely to be used in more than one state; and even within waters subject to admiralty (federal) jurisdiction, state laws are applicable to your association. With this in mind, the co-owners should agree, for the sake of clear interpretation, which state is going to govern the agreement. In this way, you will help avoid possible conflicts and expedite the settlement of any that may arise. Furthermore, should you ever need to consult a lawyer, you and your associates would know to select one who is familiar with the laws applicable to that particular state. Imagine how much legal time (and that means *money*) you would save by avoiding legal research into the laws of more than one state.

If you have ever owned a boat, you know that it requires constant maintenance and prompt repairs. Your pledge "to constantly maintain the vessel in a dependable and proudly presentable condition" cannot be taken lightly. The entire co-ownership undertaking could be defeated if one of the owners were to delay his contribution for a vital repair, one without which the boat could not operate. You see such delay in single ownership; an entire season may slip by before the boat is finally launched. Fortunately, an interdependent association couldn't tolerate such a *mañana* attitude. For this reason, some boat owners are likely to get more use from their boats in a joint ownership arrangement because of mutual insistence that their craft be ever ready, safe, and seaworthy.

The entire Interpretation clause, although it might seem at first glance to be just so much gilded gimcrack, deserves close scrutiny. It isn't a mere overture of legal terms thrown in to introduce the specific terms of the agreement; it governs the construction of the entire document. If there is a doubt about the nature of any obligation under the agreement, you will return to this clause, take a fresh bearing, and find your way. The words have been selected to strike a necessary balance between competing objectives, and as you move into the gray area of the indulgence provision, the agreement provides a gentle admonition for generosity.

As an example, you may not see any need to buy a portable charcoal grill for the boat, but one of the other owners may like to combine cruising with cooking and picnicking. For him, having that little grill on board would make a lot of difference. To "indulge" him in this small matter seems like spending peanuts compared to the savings you realize when he puts up his proportionate share of the acquisition cost, slip rental, insurance, and yard bills. And you, too, can get full use out of the grill, even though you paid only part of its cost.

But if, while indulging each other with the symbolic "few pennies yielded up," you overdo it and start to cancel out the financial benefits of belonging to the association, everyone's attitude of hearty give-and-take could begin to disintegrate. The agreement shouldn't be interpreted to mean blind indulgence of every whim that comes along, but only giving in when it comes to those little things that make a big difference.

Now, if you think this sounds like a bit of contrivance in what you would prefer to be a spontaneous part of the relationship, you are absolutely correct. It is a carefully thought-out policy for the sake of a well-balanced, happy relationship, and it still leaves plenty of room for spontaneity.

Adaptation

3. From time to time, we may wish to change the terms of our Agreement. This we may do, with our unanimous written or oral assent, subject to each owner's right to repudiate any unwritten modification and to insist on the terms of this Agreement as made or as we may in writing amend it. However, when one of us, in reliance upon a deviation from the written Agreement (whether by oral modification or tacit assent) has so changed his position that we cannot return to the written Agreement in a particular way without causing a significant monetary loss or diminution in use to that party, the oral modification or tacit assent shall govern as long as such circumstances continue.

Once executed, a contract stands immutable. Relationships, however, are constantly in flux. No matter how carefully thought out your agreement may be, you will eventually want to do some things that aren't in strict accordance with it; so you may amend it. You cannot—nor would you want to—prevent such flexibility. The agreement must therefore foresee and accommodate these changes.

Oral agreements and tacit understandings, both sure signs of a healthy relationship, are not to be discouraged either. But they can be hazardous. What happens when a conflict arises over some oral modification—when you thought you had an understanding and it turns out that you didn't? In that case, the written agreement provides the ground rules, and you must return to it. With no hard feelings! You must do so, that is, unless a return to it would, by that time, seriously impair a partner's ability to participate in the use and enjoyment of the boat.

Say, for example, that all the owners, after a discussion, moved the boat from its original berth to another location a few miles down the river for the sake of stronger winds, better fishing, or some similar advantage. All the owners except one are under the impression that the move will be temporary, lasting only a few months. But the one owner who thinks the change in berth is permanent meanwhile retires, sells his house, and buys another one in the immediate vicinity of the boat for no other reason than to be close enough to take full advantage of his scheduled time aboard. Now, if his partners say, after a few months, "Okay, time's up—let's move the boat back to the first mooring," you can safely assume that he is going to feel abused. And rightly so. The only fair thing to do is to leave the boat in its second location, even though the first place of berth is the one specified in the written agreement.

Obviously, it is better to make all your modifications in writing. For the fastidious, an annual joint review of the written agreement will surely reveal several practices that are not exactly in keeping with the written contract but that are to be continued on a permanent basis. If so, an amendment should be prepared, numbered, and attached to each owner's copy of the contract. Nothing formal is required. The following will do:

Amendment # _____

We agree to amend our joint ownership Agreement of the vessel _____ in the following particulars:

[state the changes]
This Amendment supersedes only such provisions of our original Agreement as may be in conflict with it.

Dated _____

_____ [signed]

If your attorney advises you to have the original agreement notarized, then by all means have each amendment notarized also.

With this provision in the agreement to act as chafing gear, you have the flexibility you will need to make occasional changes, both written and oral, without the danger of putting an irreparable crack in the partnership.

Terms

4. As used herein, the word *party* refers only to those who are parties to this Agreement. The singular pronoun is to be construed as either singular or plural, with the plural as either plural or singular. Masculine pronouns refer to both men and women. The terms *vessel, yacht,* and *boat* are synonymous and include the vessel's initial equipment, plus any jointly purchased additions or replacements. The term *equipment* includes machinery, outboard motors, dinghies, gear, sails, tackle, rigging, spars, furniture, utensils, trailers, cradles, and/or anything else jointly acquired that is used in conjunction with the vessel.

Look at this as one more step—tedious, perhaps, but necessary—on the way to a complete understanding of what is yours, mine, or ours. One can never be too careful in making certain that the words used in a contract have the same meaning for everyone involved; therefore, many contracts contain a provision like this to clarify the terms. It's good idea to have this written into the agreement, even though all of you may now be aware of the meaning of the terms and agree to them verbally.

Ownership

5. Each of us shall own jointly an equal, undivided share in a ___[type of boat]___ built in ___[year]___ by ___[boat builder]___ named the ___[name of boat]___ , and certified under the maritime laws of the United States [or registered in the State of _____] and titled in the name of [one or more associates], who shall hold the same for us in accordance with the terms of this Agreement.

Additional Provision for Vesting Ownership in Survivors:

We shall hold this boat as joint tenants with Common Law right of survivorship. The consideration for this tenancy is the following:

Upon the death of one of the parties and his interest passing to the survivors free of any liens, claims, debts, or demands against the deceased's interest in the vessel other than the purchase money obligation, the survivors

a. Shall pay when due the purchase money debt owed to _____; and

b. Shall pay all outstanding obligations of the deceased arising from this Agreement, provided, however, that if the total obligations of the deceased exceed the value of his interest as determined by either sale or survey, the estate of the deceased shall be liable for the excess.

The Ownership clause without the additional provision will be sufficient to vest undivided interest in the boat. However, it is not sufficient to pass title automatically to the surviving partners should one or more of the owners die.

If you plan to borrow all or nearly all of the money for acquisition, you may want the boat to transfer automati-

38

cally to the surviving owners in return for their agreement to assume and pay the entire debt after your death. Or you may simply want to give you. interest to them for the sake of affection or so that your family will not have to be concerned with the boat. If this is the case, adding the additional provision should be sufficient.

Since state laws sometimes differ in this respect, your lawyer should advise you on the consequences of any such modification and furnish you with the exact words needed to accomplish your objective in your own state. He may tell you that your state follows extremely technical rules with regard to joint tenancy that would preclude your doing it at all. Even in such a case, you could still include the language as a prefatory statement of your desires. You could also have your attorney approach the problem through your will, if you're determined to leave the boat to the surviving owners.

In the event that you elect to use the survivorship provision, the attorney may also recommend specific language for the title documents.

If you are going to be cruising in foreign countries, you will find that documenting the boat—a tedious but once-only task—cuts a certain amount of red tape when you clear U.S. ports and enter foreign ones. Documentation also saves you the necessity of annual state registration and places your boat directly under the jurisdiction of the federal government. Yet another good reason for documentation is that it makes financing easier.

Notice that the boat may be titled in all the associates' names or in one or more of their names. Using only one name on the title may save you the trouble of changing registration or documentation every time there is a change in interest. If one party already owns the boat in his name, the others could join him as co-owners; and although the boat would then be registered in his name only, he would hold it as a trustee for the others.

In our opinion, the names of all the parties who own the

boat should be on the title. But if it is more expedient for you to use only one name, you should do so only on the advice of a local attorney. Since to the world it would appear that the registered owner was the sole owner, the registered owner, in breach of his trust, *could* pass title to an innocent third party. You should either have full trust in the title owner, or you should make sure your name gets on the title documents too. On the other hand, if you can't trust the title holder, you wouldn't want to become a co-owner with him anyway.

Whether your name is on the title or not, there should be affixed to the title documents a statement similar to this one:

> The rights of the owners to use, pledge, hypothe-cate, transfer, and assign this vessel are restricted and governed by a certain Agreement, entered into on the _____ day of _____, by and be-tween _____ [owners' names] _____ .

Status of Association

6. We do not, nor shall any of us, hold ourselves out as being partners, joint venturers, or agents engaged in any combinative undertaking other than as co-owners of the vessel herein named.

Except to the extent that we may act as agents by necessity, we do not grant to each other, nor shall we assume, any powers as respective agents, other than those powers which are expressly granted by the terms of this Agreement or necessarily implied to accomplish its purposes.

To the extent an agency power is granted, it shall not be revokable until the termination of our ownership interest or until modified by written agreement; nor shall the insanity or disability of an owner revoke any attorney or agency powers.

Dual in nature, this clause further delineates the relationship for the parties and makes it clear for the rest of the world.

Among the parties, you want to define and limit the extent to which each of you can commit the others to binding agreements and do things on each other's behalf.

And as for persons outside the ownership arrangement, you want to make sure that your intentions aren't misunderstood. It is not your intention to create any type of association or partnership; the agreement simply establishes the rights of the parties to the use of their jointly owned boat. To that end, it contemplates and, for the most part, provides for separate, individual use rather than participation together as in a joint venture.

Generally, joint owners are not agents for each other, unless they expressly permit it. However, admiralty courts have a salutary doctrine, known as "agent by necessity," included here in hopes that state courts will apply the concept. It permits an owner who is then the master of the vessel to do everything that a prudent owner would do to protect the boat in time of peril.

For fear that you may be tempted to jettison the clause as mere boilerplate, we also point out another fact: it ensures that the important powers you have granted to each other cannot, except by written agreement, be withdrawn for the duration of the co-ownership.

Lien Prohibition

7. Except as herein permitted or with our unanimous consent, we shall not permit or cause the pledge, hypothecation, transfer, or assignment of any interest in the vessel. Neither shall we cause or permit any lien to attach to the vessel or to our interest in it, except as may be necessary in an emergency or to secure repairs. Any violation of this provision shall automatically terminate the right of the violator to the use of the vessel: but in no way will it relieve him or anyone

acquiring an interest through him of the duty of meeting all other obligations of this Agreement. The violator's suspended rights shall not be restored until his breach has been cured and he has reimbursed the owners for any losses they might have incurred as a result of the breach, including attorney fees, out-of-pocket expenses, and reimbursement for any loss of use of the vessel at the rate of its charter value.

Ordinarily, a property owner has a clear right to sell or borrow by pledging his property as he sees fit. But in an association like this, you can imagine where such a right could lead if one of the owners pledged his interest in the boat for a personal or business loan. You could find the boat prematurely on the auction block or involved in all sorts of legal proceedings.

One of the trade-offs of joint ownership is giving up your right to use the boat for collateral in return for the assurance that you will avoid the financial difficulties of sole ownership.

The seemingly draconian provision requiring any violator of this clause to reimburse the other owners at the going charter rate seems quite equitable, considering the inconvenience and ire any violation of this nature is likely to provoke. But primarily it should effectively discourage any partner who might otherwise be tempted to violate the prohibition.

Insurance

8. At all times during our ownership, we shall provide and maintain in full force:

   a. Hull insurance covering the yacht to full value, providing a deductible of _____;

   b. Protection and indemnity insurance, with limits in the amount of _____; and

c. Medical payments coverage of not less than
_____ per person.

The policies shall name each of us as insureds. They shall include [your cruising area] within its navigational limits and provide in-commission coverage [year-round, or during such lesser period as preferred]. He who cruises elsewhere or during the layup period shall first, at his own expense, extend the policy coverage.

The policy shall provide *inter alia* coverage for cross-liability claims among the owners.

Claims proceeds for any losses shall first be used to repair and replace that which is damaged or lost, and in case of total loss, the proceeds shall come to us as our interest may then be, after the Purser pays from the proceeds any joint debts owed to others or to each other, in the manner provided for in the clause titled Division of Proceeds.

Marine insurance is vastly different from the kind that covers the family car. Born of centuries-old shipping ventures, it comes to the modern yachtsman garbed in the quaint language of bygone eras.

If you ever needed an expert, it's here, among the complexities and seemingly archaic terms of marine insurance. "Free of capture and seizure," "barratry," "maintenance and cure," "constructive total loss"—these are samples of the phrases peculiar to maritime insurance policies.

But a knowledgeable broker, one thoroughly familiar with marine insurance, can quickly clear up any confusion as to their meaning and will explain that all the seemingly outdated terms actually carry the weight of traditional concepts as defined and used by today's courts. He can also shed some light on the reasoning behind the various types of coverage typically offered the yachtsman.

So your first move is to seek out that insurance broker and spend as much time with him as you need to understand what coverage you should have and exactly what you will get for your premium.

If your boat is anything larger than an outboard runabout, your broker will most likely advise you to get a yacht type policy rather than what is called a boatowner's policy. The true marine yacht policy generally offers better all-around protection, especially in the area of liability. The clauses that you will need to include will depend, of course, on your boat, your geographic area, and your particular circumstances. But the main portions will be for hull coverage, the protection and indemnity (P & I) clauses, Longshoremen's and Harbor Workers' Act (LS & HWA) clauses, and the medical endorsements.

The Insurance clause in the agreement requires that you insure the hull at a full, agreed-upon value. This is because your boat could be worth more than the average cash value of another one of the same size, type, and age—which, in case of a total loss claim, is what you would collect without having an agreed-upon figure.

Incidentally, if you plan to race you should make it a point to learn what the policy excludes in the way of fittings and rigging while racing, since you will have the option of including them for an additional premium.

If winter boating is possible in your area and you are inclined to take advantage of it, you may want to consider year-round in-commission coverage to maximize use of the boat. However, you can sometimes save a few dollars if the policy requires a layup during part of the year. You will want to keep in mind that many policies still exclude coverage for damage from freezing and ice, even while the vessel is moored.

The policy will also specify the geographic area within which the boat is covered. While it is foolish to buy more coverage than you need, skimping on either area or time coverage will defeat your objective to make the fullest possible use of your boat at minimum risk. On the other hand, buying year-round or worldwide coverage, then allowing the boat to hibernate all winter in port, would obviously be wasteful.

Before leaving for a foreign port subject to unstable or unpredictable governments, it would be wise not only to extend the geographic limits of coverage, but also to get additional coverage against any seizure by a foreign government—one risk that is usually excluded unless requested.

Any change in ownership, type of operation, or geographic location should be reported to your underwriter, just to make sure such a change doesn't void the policy.

One of the easiest ways to void the hull coverage and absolve the underwriter of any obligation to cover losses to the vessel, as some of us painfully learn, is by our own negligence. Hull insurance today, just as in the days of the clipper ships, protects from the perils common to the sea, not from the boat owner's negligence, however unintentional. You could, in fact, lose your coverage of the boat by doing nothing, if that means leaving her in the slip too long, neglected and uninspected. If you fail to inspect her periodically and she sinks from some undetected leak, you could find yourself without coverage.

A good cure for slovenly habits is to read the "Hull and Machinery" section of your policy; you'll probably find these or similar words: "The insurance provided by this section shall cover . . . all risk . . . providing such loss or damage has not resulted from *want of due diligence by the owners of the yacht.*" (Emphasis added.)

Remember, however, that we're talking only about the hull insurance. We're not saying that "want of due diligence" will cause you to lose coverage under the Protection and Indemnity section for damages caused to others.

This point emphasizes one of the benefits of joint ownership mentioned earlier. Used and inspected more often, your boat will be more surely protected.

Whether you own your boat jointly or not is somewhat immaterial, though, to some of the common risks of boating. Let's face it; there are definite possibilities of injury to other people. To skimp on policy limits these days is foolish. High limits and an umbrella policy are options that you should consider. Umbrella policies are those with high monetary limits that provide broad liability coverage in excess of that provided by one's underlying automobile, marine, home, and other liability policies.

If you have a trailer rig, you may want to get coverage for the trailer as well and add this sentence to your agreement:

> Each party agrees to undertake the duty of providing for the operator of the vehicle that tows the vessel, liability insurance, with single limit coverage of not less than $_____ (or its equivalent).

Uninsured Vessel Damages

9. To the extent that our vessel should suffer a mishap for which we are not otherwise fully indemnified, our liability to provide indemnification to each other shall be limited as follows.

   a. Damages to the vessel due to wear and tear, latent defects, inevitable accidents, inscrutable fault, and the joint negligence of us all, shall be regarded as our common misfortune and shall be shared by us jointly in proportion to our ownership interest.

   b. For acts or omissions pertaining to seamanship, navigation, or management of the vessel, which constitute nothing more than simple negligence, a party's liability for damage to the vessel shall be limited to a sum no greater than the deductible applicable to the hull insurance policy, or $_____. However, if the degree of culpability should constitute gross negligence, then for his heedlessness, his reckless disregard of known perils, and his indifference to consequences, a party shall stand liable for the whole or any part of any uninsured or unindemnified loss.

c. Unless he has acted in an effort to avert a greater peril, a party shall be liable for all injurious consequences which were intended or which occur during an unauthorized use or while permitting a third party to use the vessel in violation of this Agreement, including but not limited to damages to the vessel, loss of use, inconvenience, compensation for time and services expended on matters pertaining to the loss and its rectification, and all other damages provided by law and other provisions of this Agreement.

d. A party whose act or omission causes the loss or lapse of insurance coverage, or who fails to give notice of such loss or lapse of insurance as required, shall be liable for that portion of any damage to the vessel for which otherwise there would have been indemnification by an underwriter. Provided a party whose liability arises under this subsection shall not be liable to either an owner whose gross negligence or intentional wrongdoing caused the damage or one whose negligence or wrongdoing in the operation of the vessel caused the loss and he was then making unauthorized use of the vessel.

e. As between those of us who should have joint liability under these provisions, we shall be obligated to make contributions proportionate to our fault. But no contribution shall be required to be made to a party who contributed to the loss through his intentional wrong, gross negligence, or unauthorized use of the vessel.

If it's too upsetting, you can disregard any further thought as to how the cost of repairing damages to the vessel will be made up among you. In most notable cases, the insurance company will pay for them; and even if it doesn't, your own little group of owners can function as a mini-insurance company by spreading the risk equally among you.

Besides, if you have no provision regarding the matter, the law of the jurisdiction where the damage occurs will have a rule for you. Of course, you may not like the rule, since it probably wasn't made specifically for yachtsmen in the first place; and moreover, you can't be sure which rule will apply until after the damage occurs.

But by hammering out this sticky little problem in advance, you will introduce more certainty into the relationship, and you can draft a rule tailored to yachting and to your particular group's opinion as to what is fair and equitable. The exercise itself will function as both notice and warning against forbidden behavior.

It bears repeating that the major losses will, in all probability, be covered by hull insurance. Here, we are dealing only with those that remain: the noninsurables (wear and tear, deterioration, scratching and denting); the deductible portion of any covered losses; the difference, if any, in case of total destruction, between your hull insurance and the boat's true worth; liability for any mishap that results from intentional wrongdoing; and losses that occur during the absence or lapse of coverage. If you carry adequate hull insurance and avoid situations that could cause a loss or a lapse of insurance, then most of this explanation will remain an academic exercise.

Simplicity alone might suggest a clause requiring an owner to pay for any damages that occur during his use. But is that fair? Suppose, for example, you fail to make a needed repair to a stay fitting for which you were responsible and also fail to insert a warning in the log. An innocent partner takes the boat out and loses the stick. *He* should be liable? You can conjure up a flotilla of situations in which this kind of disposition would be supremely unjust.

Instead of basing liability on the vagaries of timing, the

agreement assigns responsibility for losses according to the degree of culpability in causing them.

Obviously, losses from wear and tear, the unavoidable, and joint neglect will be apportioned equitably in relation to ownership interest.

And as for your liability for simple mistakes, the usual errors and omissions that plague even the prudent are limited to reimbursement to the other owners for the deductible amount stated in the insurance policy, or a stated amount equivalent to a normal deductible.

One might argue that the negligent party should bear liability for all uninsured damage, but we disagree.

The approach to simple negligence that we have used in the agreement is, we think, more in keeping with the spirit of the association than the "tough luck" attitude. It addresses an area of common vulnerability—that of honest mistakes and poor judgment. Before you object to sharing these kinds of losses, remember that you could just as easily be sitting on one side of the boat as the other.

What if the association voted deliberately to underinsure the hull, or it became underinsured through ignorance of the boat's true worth or inflation; and then one unfortunate moment of bad judgment on your part resulted in a total loss of the boat? Certainly, it would be equitable to hold you responsible for the whole loss. But losing what you have already spent for your share of the boat is different from digging into new money to buy the remaining splinters at their previous value. By putting yourself on both sides of the issue, you can see the fairness of the lenient approach recommended by the agreement.

We have two other arguments in support of a limitation on liability for acts of simple negligence. But before advancing them, let us describe the opposite of the negligent yachtsman. He is the ever-prudent yachtsman, and if he were on your boat for long, you'd be calling him by other names that can't be printed here. By the end of the day, it's not beyond the realm of possibility that his stern would bear the imprint of a seaboot or two. You see, this guy would object to your having a martini, even with double anchors out and the season's most gorgeous sunset. ("Who knows but what we might have to get underway unexpectedly?") He would insist on an anchor watch throughout the night and a lookout in addition to a helmsman when in pilot waters. Gunkholing would be totally out of the question, since navigation would be restricted to the buoyed channel. Never would he stand idle or relax—but he'd constantly be inspecting, repairing, replacing, and reminding. As you'd expect, his judgment would always be perfect, his knowledge of all facets of seamanship complete (including federal, state, county, and town laws and regulations). He would, of course, appear to you as an officious, pompous egotist and an impossible ass. Eventually his immunity from errors and from the stresses of fatigue, fear, nausea, sleeplessness, and exposure would infect you with a fatal case of inferiority complex.

We've gone to absurd lengths to make a simple point: thank God the totally prudent yachtsman doesn't really exist. If he ever did, he'd have to own his boat alone, because no one else would share one with him for long. With the exception of racing, yachting at its best is a leisurely, relaxed sport, not the pursuit of perfection. By limiting your respective liability to each other for the simple mistakes, chances are that you will reap a better reward in understanding, forgiving, and sharing of human frailty. And there will be no tendency toward "dockside boating" for fear of having to buy the splinters.

Now, for those who are simply reckless and give no thought to your mutual interest, a harsher rule applies, for such actions are an obvious breach of trust. An example may help explain the difference between simple and gross negligence.

One of your partners—call him Sluggish Sam—is piloting the boat back to the marina through a congested harbor when he realizes that he is on a collision course with another boat some 50 meters ahead. Sam has the right of way, so he merely keeps to his course and assumes that the other boat will eventually change its direction. It doesn't. With only 30 meters between them, Sam finally hears shouts from the other boat about a broken tiller. He veers sharply to starboard, but it's too late. A crestfallen Sam returns to the dock in need of repairs to his ego as well as the gunwales. He knows that if he had been more alert the incident would never have happened.

In the same harbor on another day, we see your other partner, Hot-Spar. Having lifted the bottle some hours ago as soon as he lifted anchor, he's a full "three sheets to the wind" and having a great time racing with two other boats. He's also steering a collision course toward a fourth boat— one that happens to be dead in the water, although it isn't obvious. The last thing in the world that Hots wants to do is yield his right of way, change course, and lose the race. So he plunges ahead, at full speed, doing nothing more in the way of prevention than to yell angry warnings as the accident becomes imminent.

Both incidents could have been avoided, and indeed they should have been. But only Sam made any attempt to do so. Sleepy and tired after a long day at the helm, he suffered one of those unfortunate lapses of judgment. But Hot-Spar, the menace, exhibited an inexcusable, reckless disregard for the safety of your boat, his crew, and the other boat. He is the dangerous partner, the one who shouldn't be allowed to command anything bigger than a model yacht on Central Park Pond. (And even there, he's likely to run into trouble.) That's why we have made him totally liable to the other owners for his conduct—or misconduct, as the insurance company will call it when they attempt to reject the claim.

Intentional wrongs, of course, are criminal and obviously warrant the imposition of full liability not only for direct losses but for all related inconveniences and expenses.

The clause, we believe, is fair. It strikes a good balance between the equities and the realities of yachting. Few will

51

ever find a need to use it. But such possibilities have to be examined and, with perhaps a few personal alterations, made a part of every agreement.

Uninsured Claims

10. A party whose negligence, fault, or misconduct in seamanship, navigation, or operation of the vessel causes or contributes to the injury of a third party shall indemnify the others against any resulting uninsured claims or those amounts that exceed the underwriter's coverage.

    If a third party injury results from a deficiency in the condition of our vessel, a party shall provide such indemnification only if the injury arises out of the use of the vessel with his full knowledge of the defect and attendant dangers, but only to those among us who were ignorant of the defect and whose failure to discharge a specified duty to maintain, repair, inspect, or report a deficiency in no way contributed to the casualty.

    The foregoing notwithstanding, a party whose act or omission causes the loss or lapse of insurance coverage shall provide indemnification against any claim, regardless of cause or fault, to the same extent for which otherwise there would have been indemnification by the underwriter. In such event, a duty to indemnify imposed upon any other party shall be limited to the amount by which the loss exceeds that which would have been covered by insurance.

    As between those of us who, under the terms of this agreement, should become jointly liable to provide indemnification, we shall be obliged to make contribution proportionate to our respective fault, if that be ascertainable; otherwise, our duty to provide contribution shall be equal.

    Provided, however, that in no event shall either indemnification or contribution be required to be

made to a party who contributed to the injury through
his intentional wrongs, gross negligence, or unauthorized use of the vessel.

Some people's greatest fear of owning a boat with other
people is their exposure to liability for the negligence of the
other owners. It *seems* obvious that the risk is greatest in a
joint ownership situation. If that were true, however, surely
you would think that the increased risk would be reflected in
higher insurance rates for the jointly owned boat; actually,
the premiums charged by many underwriters are set without
regard to the number of owners.

Without insurance, of course, the risk would not be acceptable. Few of us would even think of leaving the
pier—or a garage, for that matter—without adequate protection.

In some significant ways, an ownership association can
help you reduce your personal risk by boosting the coverage you can afford. Right away, it furnishes the extra
money to get a policy with a small deductible, high limits,
and wide risk coverage. And if you're buying a boat together, the additional purchasing power may allow you to
choose a diesel engine rather than gasoline. Whenever you
read about a marina fire from now on, look to see whether it
was caused by a gasoline explosion. Is your insurance
coverage adequate to cover ten or twelve yachts that might
have been berthed nearby, as well as damage to the marina
itself? Throw in a few cases of permanent injury or death,
and the question could keep you awake nights.

We'd personally accept the additional risk of three more
owners for our boat over the risk of a gasoline-powered,
high-speed boat capable of doing 25-plus knots. To the extent that the association provides the means for a diesel
engine and the added room and comfort to enjoy cruising
rather than chasing about (without the controls of an or-
ganized race), it diminishes your risks dramatically.

Set that floating Molotov cocktail at torpedo speed, put it

under the command of a Captain Gasohol—gas for the boat, alcohol for him—and we'd gladly take the risk of ten more owners. We recognize, of course, that alcohol is an accepted, integral, time-honored part of yachting, institutionalized by the ubiquitous yacht club bar and dockside tavern. It all goes back to the era of sail, when a seaman's only fears were the sea, the lash, and missing his ration of grog.

Today, many practitioners of good seamanship make it a rule to unstop the cork only "while the hook is down." From the chilling figures compiled by the Coast Guard, though—statistics top-heavy with fair-weather collisions and man-overboard drownings—you might infer that on some boats the rule has to be "drinking permitted only while the hook is up," or worse still, ". . . anytime except while the hook is going up or down."

If you adopt some sensible rules about the booze, make sure your insurance coverage is ample and stays in effect, and indulge in a diesel engine for your choice of inboard power, chances are you'll never need to look at this clause again. Before going on to the next subject, though, a glance at its principles would be in order.

The clause deals only with claims that aren't covered by insurance. If the policy is in effect at all times and carries high upper limits, your chances of being the target of such a claim are small.

Observe also that the provision is designed to afford some ultimate protection to an innocent owner who, though practically free of fault, may be held liable because of his ownership interest.

Finally, you should realize that the clause has only limited utility, after all. It does not, nor can it, prevent your becoming liable to a third party. It does provide for your indemnification—that is, your right to reimbursement—in certain cases from another co-owner. But, following some havoc like a gasoline explosion where, say, the owner at fault is held liable for several million dollars' worth of damage in excess of your insurance coverage, could he actually pay the claim himself or indemnify the innocent owners for the share they must pay? Nothing short of megabucks or bankruptcy could get someone out of that kind of catastrophe.

Under the agreement, claims arising from the actual operation of the boat are easy to handle. Ultimate responsibility for any uninsured portion is assigned to the owner who was using it at the time of the accident. After all, that would be his liability if he were the sole owner.

For claims emanating from an unseaworthy condition of the boat, things get a bit more complicated. It would have been proper to stipulate that since the condition of the boat is your joint responsibility, no one party should have to indemnify any of the others for such claims. But that isn't really fair. If one owner knows nothing about a defect, and another owner, with full knowledge of it and the risk it entails, throws caution to the winds and uses the boat anyway, the reckless one should be made to account to the innocent owners.

But, then, suppose the partner who knew nothing about the defect was ignorant of it simply because he had neglected one of his assigned maintenance duties? In that case, the agreement does not protect the owner who was ignorant of the defect, because Mr. Careless, whose inaction contributed to the situation, shouldn't be entitled to protection from the innocent captain, or even the not-entirely-innocent one.

As between two or more guilty parties, we chose the admiralty rule of comparative negligence for the agreement. In many state courts, if two people are negligent—one very much at fault, the other ever-so-slightly—they nevertheless share the blame equally. That means that if one owner pays all the damages, he can collect 50 percent back from the other "guilty" party. Admiralty, on the other hand, apportions the damages in proportion to the parties' culpability, perhaps even to the point of acquitting a party who is only slightly at fault. Among boat owners, this rule seems to be the better one by far. If two owners are the cause of a third owner's having to pay a claim, for instance, the agreement provides that those two at fault will indemnify the third one in proportion to their respective fault.

Unathorized Use

11. No party shall ever use the vessel or permit another to make use of it when it is known to be uninsured or when his right to use the vessel has been suspended under the terms of this agreement. Nor shall any use of the vessel be made or permitted during the layup period, beyond the navigational limits specified in the insurance policy, or in any manner prohibited or excluded by the underwriter.

    The violation of this prohibition shall constitute an unauthorized use of the vessel and shall be considered a conversion of the co-owners' interest.

    In lieu of the damages and penalties afforded by law for the willful conversion of property, the innocent parties may elect to seek or accept repossession of the vessel and thereupon sell or buy the violator's interest, either at its then appraised value (for its quick sale), or at its original acquisition cost, whichever is less, with the proceeds to be distributed as herein provided for a voluntary sale. However, any balance due the violator from such sale shall be held pending the determination of any damages due from the violator because of the prohibited use and shall be applied toward the payment of such damages. From the date of the election to sell or buy the violator's interest until the transfer of his interest, the violator shall make no further use of the vessel, but his obligations hereunder shall remain unimpaired. The owners shall also recover such additional damages as may be provided by the terms of this agreement.

Nothing comes in quite so handy as a lively imagination

when drafting contracts. You try to anticipate everything: the things most likely to go wrong, the things least likely to happen, and the worst conceivable turn of events.

Financially, one of the worst things that could befall an owner is the occurrence of a serious accident while the boat is not insured. Joint ownership might work to your detriment here by creating the false sense of invincibility that often comes from belonging to a group. Put this kind of "group-think" together with the euphoria of a couple of drinks and the temptation of a beautiful day, and it's all too easy to say, "Oh, what the hell; let's go anyway—nothing's going to happen!" Whether *it* happens that way (through deliberately taking a chance) or as the result of ignorance, carelessness, or stubborn recklessness, the consequences are the same.

No contractual provision in this (or any other) owners' agreement can restrict the rights of a third party to sue all the owners jointly for injuries caused by any one of them. What it can do—and this agreement does—is make recovery from a faultless owner considerably more difficult and provide for reimbursement of the innocent by the guilty, should this protection fail. But more important, the agreement, through this clause, takes a strong preventative stance by thoroughly discouraging the use of the boat when it is not insured. Thus, the clause on Uninsured Claims requires indemnification between the owners for any such losses. But indemnification is not good enough when you consider the likely financial inability of any one owner to bear the sole burden of a formidable liability claim. As a result, one owner's right to seek indemnification from another owner will have meaning in many cases, but not in the worst. Besides, approaching the problem by merely providing for indemnification is like putting an ambulance at the bottom of the cliff rather than a fence at the top. The objective is to prevent an uninsured loss, not to tidy up the equities after one occurs. That's what this clause should do. It offers a formidable disincentive against any uninsured use and attempts to isolate the wrongdoer from the innocent owners.

The seriousness of the mere possibility calls for drastic measures. One way out is for you to turn back the clock and cease to be an owner. The agreement says that when the violation occurs (that is, the minute the boat is used under conditions prohibited by this clause) the violator becomes sole owner, by way of willful conversion: in plain language, theft.

It follows, then, that if an owner should have an accident after willfully converting the boat to himself, as its sole owner he will be solely liable for the damages. The innocent owners can then sue for the value of their interest.

For the conversion of property, the law usually treats the transgression as a sale, awarding to the rightful owner a judgment equal to the market value of the property as of the day of conversion. But that may not be fair enough to the innocent owners. Therefore, the agreement affords other remedies which, you may note, should sweeten the deal and effectively discourage any one of the owners from ever taking a chance.

There are simply too many courts in too many jurisdictions for you to be assured that this clause will, in every case, protect you from third-party claims resulting from unauthorized use of the boat. But we're willing to wager that your attorney will tell you that your chances of escape are far better with the clause than without it. Even in states where owners are held liable for the negligence of any person using a boat with the owners' permission, this clause will be strong evidence against the presumption that you ever consented to its use when it was not insured.

Notice of Insurance Cancellation

12. A party who is apprised of the lapse or cancellation of the policy of insurance providing protection to us and the vessel shall immediately, and in the most certain and expeditious manner available, give notice to every other owner.

   The failure to give such notice shall render the

delinquent liable, to the extent that the underwriter
would have been, for all losses and damages which
could have been averted by either terminating the use
of the vessel, reinstating the coverage, or obtaining
new coverage from another underwriter.

Heavy hangs the burden on any owner who gets a message
of insurance cancellation. You can't afford to delay giving
notice to the others, preferably by direct contact followed by
written confirmation. If one of the other owners happens to
be out on the boat at the time, you should try to get word to
him—even if that means enlisting the help of the Coast
Guard. Something like an island-hopping cruise in the Carib-
bean would require more ingenuity, of course, but the owners at home should have the boat's itinerary and be able to
send word to the next landfall. Obviously, the boat should
stop at the first available port and stay there until fully
covered once again.

Before the annual renewal date of your policy, the underwriter may call for a survey of the boat. To anticipate that,
it's not a bad idea to check with your agent about a month
before your renewal date to avoid the possibility of a lapse
between the expiration and renewal dates. Don't assume a
grace period without first checking with the underwriter.
You wouldn't want to ruin someone's vacation or tempt him
to stretch his luck.

You may think we're overdoing this theme with warnings
ad nauseum. After all, you could reason, how often do you
hear of an accident followed by the horrifying discovery that
the boat wasn't even insured? Not often. But like one hurricane or one fire at sea, one uninsured casualty is simply too
many. Let's face it; the financial risk can often pose a more
serious threat than the accident itself.

Lest you also come to the conclusion that we dwell too
much on the morbid or negative side of things, keep in mind
that the ultimate goal of this clause is to avoid peril, not
merely to assign liability for a failure to give notice if the boat

becomes uninsured. You avoid the danger by anticipating it. Just knowing that you will be held personally responsible for a failure to give notice will go a long, long way toward ensuring that the information will be communicated. Together with the Unauthorized Use clause and its disincentives against any use of the boat while it is not covered by insurance, this kind of legal seamanship substantially reduces the danger of an uninsured casualty.

Berth

13. We shall secure a berth for the   [name of vessel]   on the   [body of water]   at   [place]   , where she shall be kept until, with our unanimous consent, we may come to agree on another harborage.

Option for Off-season Cruising:

During the months of   [any period when the vessel would otherwise be in winter layup, or the agreed-upon season] , at the election of any number of us, the boat may be moved to southern waters.

All extra costs for such off-season use will be at the expense of the participating owners, with the nonparticipants contributing their share of only those costs that would have been incurred had no such off-season use been made of the vessel.

The participants shall first agree in writing upon the boat's itinerary, how she is to be shared, and the manner in which expenses are to be apportioned.

In choosing between an area where the boat has had previous use by any of the participants and a new area, the new area is to be preferred. In choosing between two areas where the boat has had previous use by any of the participants, that area where the vessel had its earliest previous use is to be preferred. And in choosing between new areas, the time shall

60

be divided between them, if practical, and if not, the area shall be selected by the majority of participants, with ties to be determined by chance.

The participants shall see that the vessel is returned and in commission by the end of what would have been her layup period.

All too often, the boat is purchased and delivery scheduled before someone asks, "Where are we going to keep her?" The question eventually gets resolved; but if it is done arbitrarily, the ill will that is generated could last all season.

Choosing a port is one of the fundamental tests for determining whether you have the right partners. Obviously, if one of you wants the boat for one area and the others want it for another, someone is going to be unhappy.

While this clause requires a definite consensus on the place of berth, it leaves the door open for you to change your minds at a later date if the circumstances of the association should change. You may be grateful for the flexibility, but because the location of the boat is so fundamental to its use, we think unanimous consent should be required for any change of berth (except as specified in the option for off-season cruising, when the nonparticipants wouldn't be using it anyway). The choice of berth should be made only after all participants have given careful thought to finding a harbor suitable to their mutual and individual needs.

Unanimous consent for off-season use is not required, because we feel that one party should not be able to keep the others from enjoying one of the chief benefits of joint ownership—getting the most use from the vessel. If one party doesn't like the itinerary, he doesn't have to participate in either the expedition or its expense. That is fair enough.

Of course, for lucky people in some parts of the country, there is no such thing as "off-season." Even so, you may wish to designate part of the year for cruising elsewhere.

Here's another bit of advice, for those who may be think-

61

ing about leaving the boat docked at the waterfront home of a friend or one of the owners. The idea of avoiding slip rental by using someone's private dock appeals to everyone—but that doesn't mean it works for everyone. A great deal of sensitivity is needed to keep the plan from running aground.

Considering the traffic, the likelihood of irregular hours, and the inevitable "dockside boating," a berth at a residential dock can soon annoy the homeowners. On the other hand, the restraints required to avoid the annoyance can just as soon dampen the enthusiasm of the boat owners.

If the homeowner whose dock is being used also happens to be one of the owners of the boat, there could be further problems. He could easily begin to feel—and resent—an unspoken obligation for weather protection or minor maintenance. But at the same time, he would find it hard not to feel overpossessive of the boat tied to the end of his dock. Should the other owners ever want to move it to another location, he might become stubborn. And his associates, stung by his easy, perhaps more frequent use of the boat, would become resentful. So approach the idea of a backyard berth with circumspection.

If your boat is a trailer rig, you need only modify the agreement to this extent:

> When not in use, the vessel shall be berthed upon her trailer, ready for transport, at ___[address]___ , where she is to be so kept until, with our unanimous consent, we may change the location.

You will notice that the option providing for off-season use gives the nonparticipant a break. While the boat is being used in the winter, there should be some saving of costs that otherwise would have been incurred in laying her up for the winter. The nonparticipant also benefits from the boat's continued use, which, as mentioned earlier, tends to retard its deterioration. So if you are left behind to cope with the ice and snow, you can at least take solace in the fact that your boat is being spared the same fate.

If you and your associates have in mind optional tropical use, remember that you'll need a well-ventilated boat with lots of opening ports and hatches for comfort in warmer climates. And some kind of cabin heater isn't a bad idea if you'd like to take the chill off the early spring and late fall days while the boat is in transit. Before the first tropical use, you may need to review the Rules (as provided later in the Rules clause of the agreement) so you can adopt some special ones for the new environment.

In any case, three important things will have to be settled in advance of any winter cruising: *who* will be using the boat, *where* they will be using it, and *how much* of the cost each participant should bear.

One of the owners may be in a position to use the boat for most of the winter, while one or more of the others can manage only a week or two. Since all sorts of possibilities exist, the choices should be made well in advance of the boat's departure date so you can evaluate the equity of the arrangements and adjust your personal schedules to the boat's itinerary.

By the way, this off-season option demonstrates another boon of co-boating. If you have, or plan to acquire, a boat of adequate size (with three or four other owners, numbers we have found to be ideal under varying circumstances), off-season cruising offers good vacation possibilities. Few of us have the time or the money required for long-distance voyages. But by leap-frogging (one owner cruising so far, then another taking over), the wallet stretches as your horizon widens.

Equipment

14. The equipment itemized in the attached Equipment List and any equipment that may be jointly purchased hereafter for use in conjunction with the vessel's operation and enjoyment shall be considered, for purposes of this Agreement, a part of the boat and so owned, used, and enjoyed. All replacement items shall be charged to the owners jointly.

This equipment shall be permanently stowed as indicated in the Equipment List so that each of us may immediately locate it.

To protect the vessel and its equipment, it shall be left locked at all times, with keys distributed to each of us and one key hidden on board.

The purpose of this clause is simply to establish joint ownership of the equipment, along with ownership of the boat.

You will find it essential to designate a certain location for each item of permanent equipment, for the safety of both crew and guests (see Appendix C for a sample Equipment List and stowage suggestions). This will be discussed more fully in the explanation of the Stowage clause. So well known is this fundamental dogma of seagoing life—a place for everything and everything in its place—veteran seamen may wonder at the necessity of making a special point of it. Putting this provision into the agreement gives the owners a little boost in discipline, one ingredient often found lacking in sole ownership, where the rule is harder to establish.

We previously mentioned the possibility that members of a new association might have some used gear to donate. The amount of this "junk" you have on hand may give you some idea of the collective experience of the group. If, say, out of a group of four owners, no one has anything to contribute, you might take it as a warning of a less-than-auspicious beginning.

Undoubtedly, unless it is everyone's first venture into the yachting world, some of the needed equipment will be donated by one or more of the owners. Unless the contributions are intended as gifts to the association, you should add the following proviso after the first paragraph of the Equipment clause:

> Those items on the Equipment List which are shown thereon to be owned by one of the parties shall remain the sole property of that party and subject to his removal, but only after giving reasonable notice.

And you may want to comment further on the ownership status of particular items of equipment.

The requirement to keep the boat locked when not in use reflects more than obvious prudence. It is specifically included because some insurance policies exclude coverage for theft if the boat is not kept locked. The partner who leaves the boat unlocked thus risks being held responsible for replacing any stolen articles.

If yours is a trailer rig, especially one that carries no hull insurance, you should add to the clause:

> When the vessel is upon the trailer in storage, the best available means shall be employed to see that the vessel cannot be towed away by thieves.

Maintenance

15. The boat is, at all times, to be maintained in first-class condition, outfitted as a yacht of her size, type, and accommodations should be: clean, seaworthy, ready for service, and fully equipped in compliance with Coast Guard regulations.

Option A, for yard maintenance:

> All work shall be done by the maintenance yard, with no obligation for the parties to do more than is necessary to provide normal/operational functions and adjustments and to keep her clean, to keep her gear stowed, and to keep her free from harm for lack

of emergency repair. Volunteers, however, are not to be discouraged.

Option B, for owner maintenance:

We shall maintain the boat to the fullest extent possible from our personal labor. Attached to this Agreement is a Maintenance Schedule that lists work to be done and an annual completion date for each item.

The Maintenance Schedule is divided into four parts. Part I lists those items which are to be our joint responsibility: the chores that we anticipate will take more than four man-hours and such additional chores as we shall agree to include. For the performance of these chores, we shall choose a date well in advance so that we can all be present, preferably with volunteers.

Should one of us fail to participate in the performance of a joint chore without being excused by the others, the delinquent shall pay to those who do his share a sum equal to the yard cost of performing the chore, divided by the number of parties to this Agreement: or, without the required notice to the delinquent, a substitute worker may then be hired by or for the delinquent, who shall be responsible for the cost of the labor.

Part II of the Maintenance Schedule includes the remaining layup and outfitting chores, divided into as many segments as there are parties to this Agreement, with each party responsible for the annual performance of one of the segments. The segments shall be rotated each year so that the burden shall be equally distributed.

Part III divides the boat into as many areas as there are parties to this Agreement. Each season, while in commission, an area shall be assigned to each of us on a rotating basis. Each party shall be responsible for maintaining his assigned area and its equipment in prompt repair, good order, and Bristol fashion.

Part IV of the Maintenance Schedule contains those work items which we lack the expertise to accomplish and must be contracted out for yard maintenance.

While mutual agreement, changes in the Maintenance Schedule shall be made from time to time as experience shows us what is fair, equitable, and necessary.

A delinquent shall have no further use of the boat until his share of the work is done or paid for. After seven days' notice, a substitute worker may be hired by or for the delinquent at his expense. Until the delinquent pays for such work, he shall have no further use of the vessel, and the amount owed by him shall be a lien on his interest in the boat. But in no event shall his default lessen any of his obligations under this Agreement.

A party may, if he chooses, and at his individual expense, authorize the maintenance yard to perform any of the maintenance and repair work assigned to him or hire an able substitute to take his place in the performance of joint chores.

In the event either a party or a third party is hired by or on behalf of one of the co-owners, the co-owner for whom the hire is made shall indemnify the other owners against liabilities, expenses, and costs, including attorney fees, that may arise out of the hiring.

As the owner of a boat, you have but two choices: keep the vessel seaworthy, or lay her up. Anything in between will pose a risk to your life and the lives of others and will most likely also result in the automatic suspension of your hull insurance coverage—or at least exempt the insurer from covering losses resulting from any unseaworthy condition.

In admiralty law, "seaworthiness" means a fitness for the task at hand, which makes it a fairly relative term, incapable of being defined by specifics. But in every instance, a vessel must be strong and staunch, with the proper equipment and a sufficient and competent crew for the navigational area. You may be surprised by the cases on record where an entire ship is found to be unseaworthy because of such minor faults as a missing shower handle or a doorknob that didn't work properly! We hardly need to add that this standard of seaworthiness is itself not absolute perfection; but your duty to meet it is absolute, and nothing short of perfection seems to assure its fulfillment.

With the obligation to meet this sometimes amorphous standard, maintenance is no optional matter. To enjoy the boat with a clear conscience, you will have to keep it in a constant state of repair.

Perhaps the greatest single luxury of joint ownership is being able to afford yard maintenance. For those who have little spare time—and that includes most of us—it is essential to have the major maintenance chores done professionally, as set forth in Option A. Whatever minor maladies may arise in a joint ownership, the cure seems directly proportional to the number of owners among whom the bill can be divided.

Naturally, you'll be finding a bit of leisure time while underway, or maybe during the dead of winter, or any time that boredom strikes you, when you and your partners may be willing volunteers in some of the small tasks that are so much a part of boating. If your partners are worthy of your choice in the first place, you'll have no trouble seeing the little jobs through.

But those big jobs are different. The items requiring great investments of time—cleaning, scraping, and painting the bottom; polishing or painting the hull; stripping, restripping, and repairing the mast; annual refitting, and so on—are best left to the yard, with a clear statement in your agreement to that effect.

Those who nevertheless believe they can do most of the work among themselves should use Option B. As you might have deduced, the key to successful maintenance of this kind is the continued willingness and ability of the co-owners to perform as required. The development of the Maintenance Schedule will help the partners assess the undertaking.

In addition to equalizing the workload, rotating the chores will help prevent boredom and will help assure that all partners understand the maintenance requirements of all parts of the boat.

Don't overlook the flexibility of the option for owner maintenance. One of the partners may want to pay someone to do one or several of his assigned chores. This he is free to do. His reason for joining the association in the first place could have been to take advantage of the financial savings in order to be able to pay someone else to do some of the work. The owner maintenance option also allows for a possible decline of enthusiasm for seeing the work through in person. We here venture a theoretical principle that this enthusiasm tends to vary inversely with length of ownership. Any realistic system of joint ownership must address the subject.

Whenever you hire someone to work under your direct supervision, your liability for any injury to the worker is greater than it would be if you had used an independent contractor. However, you could contract the work out and *still* end up with the liabilities of an employer if you try to control the details of the work. Whenever you decide to employ someone directly to do the work, contract with him just as you would with a maintenance yard. Specify, preferably in writing, what you want done; next establish the price or rate of pay; and finally make it clear that he is an independent contractor, free of your control or supervision. Make it known that you are interested only in the completed work. Of course, you would be wise to establish a date by which the work will be finished, with payment to be made only upon completion.

In the case of hiring a worker to perform the chores for a delinquent partner, you will note that the agreement specifies that the delinquent contract for such labor himself, or that it be obtained "for" him. To protect yourself from liability, you should insist on an acknowledgment by the substitute worker that he functions as an independent contractor or agent for the delinquent.

Utilization

16. Our ownership of the vessel shall be joint, but our use of it shall be separate and independent.

However, during the first thirty days of ownership, we shall make maximum joint use of the boat, our purpose being to learn the ways of our vessel, to establish the best procedures for handling and caring for her, to develop common methods, to learn what we expect from each other, and to agree upon places for stowing the gear.

Following this shakedown period, the week shall be divided into weekdays and weekends, and each day and each weekend shall be allotted separately on a rotating basis. For our purposes, a weekend is from noon Friday until noon Monday, and a weekday is from noon of the assigned day until noon of the following day. The boat shall then be for the exclusive use of the assigned party as if he were owner *pro hac vice,* with no one else to be aboard except by invitation, or for emergencies.

Assignments will be made annually, in January, so that we may plan our personal calendars well in advance. Our objective in scheduling is to make optimum use of the vessel and see that each party benefits to the greatest extent possible. When one party ascertains that he will not use the boat during his allotted time, he shall so notify the others: if more than one of us wants to use the vacated period, the boat shall be used jointly, if possible, or assigned separately by lot if not. The party accepting such use shall not thereby forfeit any part of his own scheduled use.

Each of us shall have the right to one cruise annually, extending through two consecutive weekends, plus the intervening weekdays, to be exercised:

a. Only during the months of [any three or four months that exclude prime boating time for your area];

b. With at least thirty days' notice to the others; and

c. When one of the two desired weekends is already assigned to the user.

Furthering our objective, we shall try to combine vacation cruises so that one party may journey to a particular destination during his vacation and another party may use his vacation to bring the vessel home.

This clause is subject to quite a bit of variation in each association. Not only do the circumstances of each owner come into play, but the geographic area of use is a consideration as well. The foregoing suggested paragraphs serve our own family and our partnership well.

The old expression ''Different ships—different long splices'' reminds us that the methods of keeping literally dozens of things, from lines to logs, can be peculiar to each vessel but must be consistent between the gunwales. This is for the sake of sanity as well as safety. So the initial thirty-day shakedown period remains a sound practice for all fledgling associations and existing ones with new boats.

Of equal importance to the owners is the designation of intervals when they can regard the boat as their own, free to invite or exclude whomever they please, without feeling the least bit compelled to include any of the other owners. The phrase "owner *pro hac vice*" is included for legal purposes and means that the person who is assigned the boat's use is deemed the sole owner for that particular occasion.

Since weekends are, as here defined, three days in duration, the rotation of weekdays will result in the same person's getting the boat on the same day of the week if there happens to be an even number of owners. This you may or may not want. As an alternative, you could assign the days by chance. Or, if one owner always wants the boat on a certain day of the week, and it doesn't matter to the others, you could assign that particular weekday to him and rotate the others. Should your assigned weekday fall on a Thursday or a Monday when your weekend comes up for rotation, you have the bonus of a long weekend with the boat at your disposal.

Now, you may not envision enough weekday demand for the boat to make weekday assignments at all. Yet some kind of system is advisable; whenever you do see your way clear to use the boat during the week, you'll have the means to plan ahead without the bother of telephoning all the other owners.

Whatever system you adopt, make sure that it will result in equitable assignments, consistent with your mutual needs, and that it provides enough advance notice so that adequate plans can be made.

The prohibition of vacation assignments during prime boating time works well in our area of the country around the Chesapeake Bay. Summer here is not prime time for the rag haulers. Spring and fall produce the best sailing conditions on the Bay, and we want everyone to have as many chances as possible to enjoy these too-short seasons. That leaves the summer for cruises to other waters.

But, again, this matter depends on your area and your desires. If you live someplace like Florida, you may want to eliminate any such provision altogether. In fact, your needs may call for an assignment system entirely different from the one suggested here, such as assigning the boat on a weekly or a monthly basis. But if you lead a busy life on a tight schedule, shorter time divisions are probably more consistent with reality.

In our experience with two other very busy partners, we found that having the boat every third weekend and every third weekday gave us more "boat time" than we could use. In fact, during the ten years we have jointly owned a boat, we can remember only two times when we wanted the boat and couldn't get it. Even with three owners, the boat was at her mooring more than we would have liked. Unless you have both the time and the compulsion to use your boat over 50 percent of the time—a luxury that few boat owners can afford—you will be able to fit in at least one partner (thereby saving you half the cost) without diminishing your use of the boat whatsoever.

Ship's Officers

17. During the shadedown period, a Captain shall be elected for each cruise. Thereafter, unless we most clearly agree on another, he who has the scheduled right of use shall be Captain, even if others of us are then on board.

Each January, ship's billets shall be filled, with each co-owner eligible to hold more than one office, but with no obligation to accept the same position for more than one year until that office has, in the interim, been held by all other co-owners. The standing billets are:

a. *Purser:* who shall open a checking account in a jointly chosen bank, which is to be used exclusively for our purposes. He shall make (or reimburse for) all authorized purchases, keep the records, prepare the annual use schedule, make a budget for the coming calendar year, promulgate a cash-need anticipation schedule, and order the payment of assessments as needed, giving thirty days' notice whenever possible. The budget and the anticipation schedule shall be submitted to the owners and deemed adopted unless the Purser is notified of objections within 15 days of its submission, and/or amendments are made by the majority.

An assessment made to meet an obligation specified in this Agreement, or made in accordance with an adopted budget or to meet the terms of the purchase money debt or other joint obligation which pertains to the acquisition, ownership, or operation of the vessel, shall not be subject to modification unless the assessment is less than is required to fulfill its purpose.

b. *Bosun:* who shall determine and report the need for repairs, replacements, and work. The replacement of or addition to existing equipment necessary for the preservation of the boat's lawful and safe operation may be ordered by the Bosun, or if immediately needed, by any party, without further concurrence. Additional equipment may be ordered or purchased only with the consent of all. If the boat is to be owner-maintained, the Bosun will also keep a list of any necessary chores not included in the Maintenance Schedule or done by the yard. The list will be written in the Log, and we each shall obligate ourselves to see to these tasks as equitably as possible. He who completes a job will sign his name beside its entry, so that a tally may show the equitability of our relationship.

c. *Chief Engineer:* who shall obtain and study in great detail the operating and shop manuals for the motor or engine. He will post an Engine Checklist and see to the maintenance and upkeep of the engine by ordering work and replacement parts when needed to maintain the boat in good operating condition.

The problem with having a committee-captain is that group decision making is better at creating than responding to a disaster. The only time a vessel commanded by a committee is certain to survive is when they are trying to scuttle it. Because some situations demand fast decisions and clear orders, every outbound crew obviously must have a single captain.

Whether you choose to assign a captain by rotation or by natural gravitation to the most experienced seaman on board, be sure that whenever the boat leaves the dock everyone knows for sure who is boss. And rotation isn't such a bad idea. If you don't like the way the captain commands the vessel, you can always even things up when it's your turn.

In times of crisis, however, you want the most competent person in command. If there is a great disparity of experience, it is best to agree that while one party is captain, the most experienced of the owners may take over during an emergency.

Operational Care

18. The Captain shall be responsible for the performance of those repairs needed to prevent further damage and for chores necessary to keep the boat clean and her gear properly stowed. The vessel is to be returned to her mooring in a clean and neat condition, with her water and fuel tanks topped off.

There's no need to explain the rationale for this clause, but you may want to define further a "clean and neat condition" in your list of Rules to be kept posted aboard the boat.

Although you wouldn't expect infractions of these housekeeping courtesies to break up an otherwise sound partnership, they would most certainly cause a bit of vexation. The careless boating partner must discipline himself in yet another boating fundamental and learn not only to pick up after himself, but to clean up as well. As in the discipline of proper stowage, safety enters the picture. Ultimately, too many cigarette butts in the cockpit scuppers or cracker crumbs in the bilges tend to have a devastating effect on buoyancy.

Here again, trailer rigs call for a slight change in the agreement as written. In place of the last sentence of the clause, you should insert something like this:

> After each use, the vessel should be returned in a clean and neat condition, properly cradled on the trailer, with all gear secured from chafe and road vibrations and protected against marring, denting, scratching, or unnecessary wear and tear.

Rules

19. We shall faithfully abide by the attached Rules and such others as may hereafter be adopted with the concurrence of all, but with none to be in conflict with either the terms or objectives of this Agreement.

By working up the Rules together before you sign the agreement (or even buy the boat), you will know whether you all have the same objectives, and thus you will have a better measure of compatibility. Appendix B contains a sample set of Rules for jointly owned boats.

Rules should cover these subjects: equipment operation; boat cleanup; engine procedures; and reporting of damage, malfunctions, and other deficiencies (so that another owner does not unwittingly take the boat out in a hazardous condition). You may want to include an emergency checklist and other operational reminders. In fact, you could, in time, expand your Rules to become a sort of custom-tailored reference manual.

When the shakedown period is over, you may want to reword your initial Rules somewhat as you and the other partners agree on the best common methods for using the boat. If you should take on any new partners at a later date, the Rules will help introduce him to the ways of the association.

Ship's Log

20. We shall faithfully maintain a Log, with an entry for each day of use, duly signed or initialed by the Captain, who shall include the engine-on time in the margin and any necessary warnings in bold print. Dates of engine maintenance and repairs shall also be recorded.

Whatever else may flow from the captain's pen to reflect his day—poetic musings, raw humor, perhaps terse epigrams—the items of business mentioned in the provision must be recorded in the log.

This little task is considered good practice in all boating. But often the sole owner who thinks he can keep all the details in his head never bothers with a log—to the detriment of his boat's engine. In a joint ownership, it is all but impossible to keep up with the engine maintenance without records. So essential is this aspect of log keeping, for the sake of safety and top engine performance, that it is included in the agreement instead of being left to the Rules.

Rather than regarding this as an additional chore of joint ownership, you should look upon the requirement as another advantage of the relationship, one that will no doubt keep your boat in better condition than many solely owned ones.

Stowage

21. We shall permit between-cruise stowage of only the ship's gear. Any nonperishable items of food or beverage left aboard are to be regarded as abandoned and may be consumed or jettisoned by others.

You may prefer to begin this clause with a sentence like this: "Each party shall be assigned a locker for the storage of such personal items as he elects. Otherwise, we shall permit . . ." That's all right if the boat is large enough to accommodate such an arrangement and the added weight doesn't concern you, or if you keep the boat on a mooring and need to avoid a lot of rowing back and forth in the dinghy. But the average yachtsman never seems able to find enough uncluttered, readily accessible storage space for some of the things that need to stay on board. If you allow more accumulation than the boat can afford, so many items will find their way on board, that in no time at all you'll be able to measure the passage of time by the depth of the waterline.

It almost goes without saying that stowage of personal gear aboard a trailered rig should be forbidden. The mess and damage from breakage and road vibrations can do in your boat as effectively as a hurricane.

Far from being the nitpicker it would seem, this stowage clause is of utmost importance to the safety and comfort of those on board. Given free reign, a single family can bring aboard enough gear in one season to make an average size hooker ride well below her lines, and it would take nothing less than the QE2 to accommodate the unrestrained clutter of several families. Left to litter a companionway during an emergency, the innocuous radio, shoe, or book becomes saboteur as surely as Poe's black cat.

The sole exception to this antilitter clause that we find acceptable is nonperishable food and drink—provided that everyone clearly understands such items left on board to be gifts to the others, not private stock, and that the boat is not on a trailer. Even this can cause difficulties at times, as we learned a few years ago while cleaning and readying a jointly owned boat for sale. In the galley we found no less than five economy-size bottles of Tabasco sauce! The following provision was quietly slipped into the Rules for our next boat: "In order to maintain buoyancy, Tabasco sauce will be strictly limited to one-half the vessel's displacement." Our partner with the hot tooth gamely acquiesced.

Specifically, nothing should be left on the boat that isn't available for joint use, and then only when it is something likely to be needed. The Equipment List itemizes the gear that stays on board.

Third-Party Use

22. At such times as none of us desires to use the vessel, we may, with our unanimous consent, permit others to use the boat, but only those who have the requisite skill, who know the boat well, and who have rendered a service to the care and maintenance or of value to the vessel. In this case, we, the owners, shall jointly share such losses as may not be made good by the third party or the underwriter.

     Chartering of the vessel is alien to our purpose. But if a party to this Agreement should default in his financial obligations, the remaining parties may, with their unanimous consent, enter into a charter party agreement for either bareboat, voyage, or time charters. The proceeds from such charters will be applied to the upkeep of the vessel as needed, with the excess, if any, to be divided among only those parties who are not in default.

     Provided, however, before entering into any charter agreement the participating owners shall see that the insurance is extended to cover the venture.

You may want to permit some third-party use, as provided

in the first paragraph of the clause, to reward those who work on your boat or permit you to tie up at their dock. But we would advise against extending the privilege beyond those few who meet the criteria in the clause.

Boats differ greatly in their handling and equipment. And, as many people who have owned more than one boat will tell you, some damage is usually done to an unfamiliar boat, its motor, or its equipment, the risk of such damage being higher during the get-acquainted stage. Because of this, most knowledgeable people would be reluctant to use an unfamiliar boat in the absence of the owner. Those who show no trepidation over the prospect may not be very knowledgeable.

As long as things are going well financially, charters should be prohibited for the sole reason set forth in the second paragraph. But in the event a partner does default, the nondefaulting partners should at least have the latitude to minimize their losses and obtain the greatest possible benefit from their undertaking. On the other hand, if the boat is free often enough to consider a charter, why not consider an additional partner instead?

The type of charter depends on just how much control of the boat the owners want to relinquish. Under a bareboat charter, the party who takes the boat assumes complete responsibility for the navigation, operating expenses, and legal liabilities connected with the boat. The owners, in effect, hand over almost total control of the boat to the user. During time and voyage charters, the owners retain far more control, but with far more liability to others.

We will add one more warning here—about the dangers of losing your insurance coverage if you charter your boat. This is one clause of a typical yacht policy:

> Warranted that the Yacht insured will be used solely for private pleasure purposes. In the event that the Yacht is chartered, hired, leased or otherwise employed in a commercial manner, *this insurance shall terminate as of the time of*

agreement to so employ the Yacht, unless permission is endorsed hereon.

Before even deciding to charter, it would be advisable to confer with your insurance underwriter and a charter agent and also to invest an hour or two with an admiralty lawyer for a quick run-through on the ramifications of such a move. Under no circumstances should you even agree to a charter without first notifying your insurance underwriter and obtaining proper coverage. And by all means, make certain that the boat meets all pertinent Coast Guard regulations.

Guests

23. The Captain may permit guests on board, but under no circumstances shall any of us when Captain carry a passenger-for-hire or require a guest to contribute anything of value toward the expenses of a cruise.

    With the Captain's permission, guests may participate as volunteer crew members in a social capacity. However, at no time shall the operation of the vessel be delegated to anyone lacking experience and competence in the handling and operation of a vessel of the general type and size of our yacht, and at no time shall the Captain abrogate responsibility for the operation of the vessel.

    The Captain is responsible for damages to the vessel arising from the acts and omissions of guests while acting as voluntary crew, to the same extent as if their acts had been committed by him. He is also liable to indemnify us for the uninsured portions of any claims made by his guests. However, the Captain shall have no duty to indemnify any one of us who causes or contributes to the injury out of which the claim arises by failing to give prior warning to the Captain of an unseaworthy condition, by personally committing a negligent act or omission in the operation or management of the vessel, or who should be the sole or intentional cause of the tortious act.

Provided, however, though permitted by the Captain, a guest invited by another of us shall not be deemed a guest of the Captain; and as to any claims made by such a guest, the party who invited the guest shall have the same duty to indemnify against as if he were Captain.

You may be surprised that we would recommend something that seems so clearly against your best interests as to refuse an offer to help with the expenses of a cruise. Not only do we recommend it; we insist on your including this provision in your agreement. If you don't, you may one day be even more surprised at what is happening to you.

Briefly and simply, here is the reason. Any passenger who pays or gives something of value to you as captain, to anyone on your behalf, to the operator of your boat, or to another owner of the boat, either directly or indirectly, is considered—in the eyes of the law—a "passenger-for-hire." In order to carry a passenger-for-hire lawfully, you must hold a Coast Guard operator's license. Courts have been known to regard the captain and crew without one as unqualified. Whenever a vessel puts to sea (that is, leaves the dock) with an unqualified crew, she is considered unseaworthy, no matter how shipshape she may otherwise be. But the problem is more than mere insult to boat and crew. Following this maelstrom to the bottom, we find that whenever you "put to sea" in an unseaworthy condition, you risk losing your insurance coverage. We're not talking only about hull coverage. If you review the typical policy clause quoted in the explanation of the Third-Party Use clause, you'll see that you jeopardize liability coverage as well.

The Coast Guard has good reasons for requiring an operator's license of anyone carrying a passenger-for-hire. Such regulations protect the public from tour operators who would endanger lives by piloting without the requisite skills or the boat inspections required by an operator's license. But on rare occasions, some unwary pleasure boat owner has found himself, to his utter disbelief, swept into the net of this regulation, an innocent part of the catch left to do flip-flops in some court of law without any insurance protection.

Again, we recommend that you include this clause in your agreement and abide by it. But, at the risk of confusing you, we urge you not to overreact, either. What you want to avoid is any form of compensation in a business sense, as distinguished from mere social benefit or incidental contribution. You don't have to refuse the ordinary social amenities arising naturally during a cruise, as long as you don't ask for or enter into an agreement for payment or contributions. If a guest wanders into the marina store while you are refilling your tanks and comes back with pretzels and beer for everyone, that's fine. You don't have to start pouring the booze overboard as all hands stand by in thirsty wonder.

The second paragraph of the Guests clause deals with the helping hand you're bound to need from time to time. You're hot, you're tired, and you've been at the helm for hours. You need a quick trip into the cabin to check the chart and go to the head. Do you dare relinquish control to one of the guests sitting in the cockpit and leave for a couple of minutes? Common sense dictates the answer to that one. To leave the vessel in the hands of an inexperienced guest for a quick dash below in calm, uncongested waters is one thing; going below to take a nap is quite another. Just remember that when you are captain, the responsibility remains yours.

Basic to the clause is the unrestricted privilege of each owner, when captain, to act as if he were the sole owner. In the matter of guests, whom he shall ask aboard, when, where, and to what extent they may participate, are at his sole discretion. Coupled with these benefits, of course, are the responsibility for damage done by his guests and the ultimate liability for their injury.

We have provided that, unless another owner is clearly at fault, the person who invites a guest aboard shall indemnify the other owners for the uninsured portion of any claims asserted by such guest. This is because an injured guest may assert a claim against all the owners, predicated on a joint ownership obligation such as the duty to keep the vessel in seaworthy condition. If this happens, you may not even know the guest. Even if you do, you weren't responsible for his being aboard, and you were no more responsible for the faulty condition of the boat than the owner who invited the injured party. So it seems only fair that the other owner, who has equal responsibility for the seaworthiness of the vessel, should bear the ultimate risk for his personal guest.

There is another practical reason for holding a captain responsible for claims brought by his guests. Suing a group of strangers isn't the same thing as suing a friend. Tommy Tipplers and Accident Annies aren't as likely to sue for or attempt to collect more than the insurance covers if they know that their friend, the captain, will have to reimburse you for anything you have to pay. A provision like this has made the difference in many cases.

And now is as good a time as any to reemphasize the importance of writing any warnings of defects into the log and of noting any such warnings that might have been entered into the log by the previous user.

Paid Crew

24. No person shall be hired as master or crew member, on either temporary or permanent basis, unless we first give our unanimous consent, secure the necessary insurance coverage, and deposit with the Purser a sum equal to at least one month's wages of said master or crew member, plus all other anticipated expenses for one month in connection with such crew. Should the account drop to less than one-half of this required sum, the Purser shall discharge the crew with two weeks' notice.

    The responsibility for the operation of the vessel

shall not be delegated to any person lacking either license qualifications or experience and competence in the handling and operation of a vessel of the general type and size of our yacht.

Any one of us, may discharge a crew member at any time if such crew member fails to act as required or if the insurance policy does not provide general liability coverage for paid crew, including coverage for maintenance and cure, Workmen's Compensation (if applicable,) Jones Act, and Admiralty liability.

You may want to prohibit a paid crew altogether. In that case, simply change the second comma of the first sentence of the clause to a period and stop the clause right there. But you may later find a need for a delivery crew, and if you leave the clause in, it will then serve as a reminder to check insurance, secure the funds, and check crew licenses.

The requirement of a deposit of one month's wages for a paid crew represents no more than sound business sense, as practiced by many small firms that keep on hand the following month's overhead. But even without a paid crew, you may want to consider depositing a month's anticipated maintenance expenses with the Purser.

If you hire a captain, even for a very short period of time, it is essential that he have a Coast Guard operator's license. As suggested in the discussion of the Guests clause, few yachtsmen appreciate the range of possible consequences of entrusting the vessel to an unlicensed operator.

In the event of an injury to a member of your crew, under admiralty law you have the legal responsibility to care for him, see him through any disability, and perhaps pay damages to him because of some unseaworthy condition or negligence on your part. This is true whether you own a boat by yourself or with others. In the event of his death, you would be vulnerable to an action brought by his estate. And of course, as owner, you are liable for injury due to unseaworthy conditions and, subject to certain limitations peculiar to admiralty, the negligence of your paid crew. We say this only as a reminder to check for full insurance coverage.

Before you let these warnings frighten you away from co-ownership, remember that these risks are present even if you are a sole owner, and they *are* insurable. In a multiple ownership, as suggested earlier, you can get double, triple, or even more insurance coverage (depending on the number of owners) for a fraction of the price you would pay if you were the only owner. Keep in mind also that you pay less for additional coverage than you do for the initial coverage.

Granted, in theory there are greater risks in co-ownership than there are in single ownership. But to some extent your association is a small insurance company, spreading the risk among you. And, again, the fact that premiums charged by many underwriters are the same for joint owners as for solo yachtsmen suggests that the risks are comparable.

Payment of Assessments

25. We shall pay all assessments, including those for delinquent work and indemnification obligations, by the date set by the Purser. If one should fail to meet his obligations in this regard:

     a. Any other party may pay the sum in default, in which case it shall be deemed a loan to the delinquent (but not a cure of his default), payable on demand, with interest at ____%, plus expenses, including legal fees incurred in collecting; or

     b. Those who are not in default may borrow the money without such action being deemed a cure of the delinquent's default (and may even pledge either the vessel or the defaulter's interest in such as collateral) and apply the proceeds to the delinquent's obligation. In such event, the delinquent shall pay the loan when due or pay immediately the party or parties who pay the loan, including interest and all loan fees, with interest, from the date of payment, at the same rate as the loan, plus expenses, including any legal fees incurred in collecting; or

c. Those not in default may declare the sum due and immediately sue the delinquent for the sum in default, plus interest in collecting. Such action, however, shall not terminate or suspend either the Agreement or the defaulting party's obligation to perform all other duties required of him; or

d. The parties not in default or those who pay or borrow on behalf of the defaulting party shall have a lien on the interest of the party in default.

From the date the assessment is due until the same is paid, or until the delinquent repays the money loaned or borrowed on his account, he shall be deemed in default, and his right to use the boat shall be suspended. His right to participate in any decisions concerning the vessel shall likewise be suspended, but in no way shall his obligations under this Agreement terminate or abate. If the default is not made good within sixty days, the other parties, if they elect, may sell the delinquent's interest in the boat, or any number of them may buy his interest, at a price and on the terms that they judge to be the best available for an expeditious sale. In such case, this Agreement constitutes a Power of Attorney wherein the delinquent does hereby empower the other parties jointly and/or severally to do on his behalf any and all things pertaining to the sale and transfer of his interest.

The delinquent shall be duty-bound to execute such documents as may be required by those not in default to perfect the provisions of this clause. In case of the refusal of the delinquent party, the non-

defaulting parties jointly or severally are empow-
ered, as his attorney in fact, to execute the required
documents.

In no event shall this provision be construed as a
requirement for the sale of the delinquent's interest
to a third party who is unacceptable to the remaining
parties.

In spite of the effect all this jargon must have on the
average person outside the legal profession, this clause does
not complicate things. On the contrary, it is designed to
simplify matters in case of financial failure or emergency; in
self-defense, we assure you that it could easily have been
doubled in size with legalese.

We've tried to give the nondefaulting parties as many
options as possible and a broad latitude in obtaining operating funds and requiring compliance by a defaulter.

You may notice that the Payment of Assessments clause
does not handle defaulters gently. With all due respect for
the many exigencies of life, the agreement must nevertheless
protect those owners who honor their obligations and discourage those who might ignore theirs, were it made easy for
them to do so.

This is the place to mention one blind spot in joint ownership. Selling a boat is one thing; selling an interest in a boat is
quite another. The buyer of a boat gets the whole boat. The
buyer of an interest gets a boat, plus the other owners and all
the strings attached. The market for an ownership interest is
considerably smaller than that for the whole boat. If you
default, you can't expect an independent appraiser to use
the fair market value of the whole boat as a basis when
determining the value of your interest, especially when a
quick sale is needed and where the market is limited to
people who are compatible with the other owners. The fact
is, the nondefaulting owners could run an ad for a couple of
weeks for the highest offer, then assign a minimal value to
your interest and buy it themselves for a pittance.

It's harsh treatment, but fair. The soft spot is found in a later clause, where worthy hardship cases are given ample relief. Here, we deal with the broken promise. We favor those who are true to their undertakings and provide a message to those who are not: Don't default!

Sometimes anchors slip and new moorings need to be found—on land as on sea. And sometimes partnerships, even close friendships, are put to the test. Through mutual regard for the boat as well as for the sake of friendship, the co-owner in hazard of a default will do well to get off a distress signal early enough to allow for other alternatives. Then his plight is more likely to be received with compassion and reason. But if he waits until all parties are threatened, anger and the need for an immediate solution will invoke the use of this clause.

Sale of Vessel

26. Only with unanimous consent may the vessel be sold within two years of acquisition. Thereafter, it may be sold upon the request of 50% of us, but not within one year of admitting a new co-owner.

    Without unanimous consent, a party may not sell his interest within the first year of acquiring it, unless his circumstances so change as to manifest a likely inability to continue to meet the obligations of this contract or make practical use of the vessel.

    For a period of thirty days after notice of the establishment of the terms of sale of either the boat or a party's interest in it, interested co-owners shall have the right of first refusal to buy the boat. Any change in the terms of sale shall constitute a new offering, thereby creating a new ten-day period for the right of first refusal.

    In no event may a party transfer (or enter into a valid agreement to transfer) his interest to one who has not first in writing obtained the unanimous approval of the other co-owners. Nor shall a transfer become valid until all defaults by the retiring owner have been cured, or until arrangements acceptable to the co-owners have been made for their satisfaction. As a further prerequisite for the transfer of ownership, the new owner shall become a party to this Agreement and assume (or satisfy the retiring owner's *pro rata* share of any) joint liability for mutual obligations either secured by or arising from the acquisition, ownership, or use of the vessel. Any cost incidental to the transfer shall be borne by the new owner.

While the consent to purchase will not be unreasonably withheld, a candidate may be rejected for want of either seamanship abilities or financial strength. Furthermore, the nature of this relationship mandates that the personality of the party proposed be unanimously acceptable to the remaining owners, who, in this regard, shall be the sole judge.

The provisions of this section pertaining to the rights of co-owners to buy a seller's interest, the co-owners' approval of a sale to a new co-owner, and the requirements of a valid transfer, are applicable to any sale authorized anywhere in this Agreement.

Any sale or transfer in derogation of this Agreement shall be void.

This clause is fairly self-explanatory. It establishes an owner's right to sell the boat as well as to sell his own interest under circumstances we think to be fairest to everyone involved.

The objective here is to provide the flexibility to terminate the ownership or to change participants without imposing an unwanted association on the owners who remain or causing any of the parties the unnecessary economic hardship and inconvenience of a short-lived association.

One might opt for permitting only the sale of an individual's interest, or restricting the right of fewer than all the owners to sell the entire boat. However, given the propensity of boat owners for change and the more substantial market for whole boat sales, it seems to impose no great burden to allow half the owners to call for a sale—provided they take into consideration the appropriate number of years for holding the boat. A small boat purchased in May of one year for learning purposes could be sold six months later without a disproportionate amount of hardship. For a cuddy cruiser, a holding period of eighteen months might do. But a forty-four-foot aft-cabin sloop that requires a broker's services or considerable sales effort by the owners isn't the sort of boat one wants to vend on a regular basis. With a boat of that size, especially a new one purchased by the owners of an earlier syndicate, a three- or four-year required holding period wouldn't be unreasonable.

As a rule, boat ownerships change rapidly. But it would hardly be fair to decide to sell the boat out from under a new owner before he has had a chance to acquire his sea legs or an opportunity to enjoy the enterprise. A waiting period in this case seems only proper.

The practical sequence ordinarily goes something like this. When one owner in a successful association starts pushing for a sale of the boat, either the others will join him or he will settle down to wait until the others are ready to sell also. Companionship will influence him more than the desire for change, all other things being equal. But if things haven't been going well in the association? *Everyone* will want out as soon as it can be done practically and economically.

Some may feel this clause is too lenient. We can only counter by saying that we believe the important affairs of life (foolishly, at times) must take precedence over a responsible person's pleasures. Since the underlying principle of this agreement is simply the perpetuation of friendship through understanding and accommodation—with the harshest of terms for those who should prove unfaithful—a charitable approach is taken toward life's vicissitudes.

91

This provision cushions the stringent terms of the default provisions and encourages an owner to make his money problems known so that a new owner for his interest can be found before a default actually occurs. The "tough luck, buddy" response to an associate who has lost his job, or who must leave the area to care for an ailing parent, has no place in the association. Instead, the other owners surely will want to help him sell his interest. By the same token, their reaction should be no different if he got a better job or a promotion that required him to move away.

That's why the agreement permits the immediate sale of an owner's interest under any circumstances that would prevent his full participation. No one is going to turn down the offer of a handsome promotion in some distant city and stick around just so he can fulfill his maintenance obligations. The clause simply recognizes the practical, the realistic, and the reasonable.

The rights to buy a departing owner's interest and to approve the new purchaser do limit the market and make the sale of an ownership interest cumbersome and difficult; but both privileges are too important to the remaining owners to be abandoned.

In the matter of taking additional or replacement owners into the association, committing to paper any kind of definite procedure is tricky. But with all this talk of fairness, the situation calls for some guiding principles. The clause, while recognizing that an owner may have a valid and urgent need to sell his interest, nevertheless protects the rights of the remaining owners to approve—or disapprove—the potential partner.

Earlier, we expressed faith in the owners' ability to function together happily under this arrangement, regardless of differences in life style and personality. This was intended to counter the fears of those who equate sharing a boat with sharing a foxhole. However, it's one thing for partners to be different in personality or background, and it's quite another for them to be personally objectionable to one another. If one of the owners finds the character or personality of a proposed new owner to be objectionable, by no means should he be forced to make that person a part of the association.

Division of Proceeds

27. We shall share in the proceeds of any sale authorized by this Agreement by first paying lien creditors, including the liens of co-owners who have paid sums on a delinquent's default. Then our joint ownership-related debts owed to others are to be paid, with the balance to be disbursed according to our then existing interests.

Proceeds from the sale of one party's interest shall be applied *pro-rata* in the same manner, subject to modification in the contract of sale specifying the purchaser's assumption of the seller's obligations if the sale is otherwise approved by the other co-owners.

In splitting up the proceeds of a sale in a partnership, debts owed to joint creditors are usually given precedence over the debts owed by the partners to one another. But, in spite of our occasional use of the word *partner,* you are not partners in the legal sense. You are co-owners. This is an ownership association, not a partnership, and nowhere in the agreement itself will you find yourself called "partner."

As a co-owner under this agreement, you would have a lien for sums of money actually paid by you or held by you for payment to joint creditors. There is nothing wrong or unfair in *attempting* to give yourselves this preferred status. Do not be surprised, though, if your courts reject the preference and put you in line behind some of the other creditors.

Death or Disability

28. For our purposes, "permanent disability" shall mean any anticipated incapacity to use and enjoy the vessel for a period in excess of one boating season [or one year, if there are no seasonal limitations], resulting from a physical or mental illness or injury.

We shall pay or assume all expenses which are incurred after the death or permanent disability of a co-owner, with no additional assessments against such party or his estate for such expenses thereafter incurred.

In the event of the death of a party and his interest passing to his estate, or in the event of the permanent disability of a co-owner, the other co-owners shall, regardless of the length of time the vessel has been held, arrange for the sale of the deceased or disabled co-owner's interest or, at their election, arrange for the sale of the boat. The legal representative for the deceased or the disabled co-owner or his representative shall execute all documents essential to consummate the sale in accordance with the terms established by the other party or parties to this Agreement.

The disabled party or the representative of the deceased or disabled party may reject the sale, but following rejection and until an acceptable sale is made, the disabled party or the estate of a deceased party must resume paying his *pro-rata* share of all fixed expenses (i.e., those which would be incurred even if no use were made of the vessel).

The disabled party or the estate of a deceased party may vote to compel the sale of the vessel if, by the terms of the Agreement, the disabled or deceased party would then have had that right. But in no other way may the disabled person, the estate of a deceased party, or the legal representative of either participate in any decision pertaining to matters covered by this Agreement: and in no event shall the right to the use or possession of the boat pass to any such third person, or to the estate, heirs, legatees, legal representatives, or assigns of a party.

Provided a disabled party who is legally competent to do so may personally reject the status of a disabled party and continue as a party to this Agreement with all the rights and duties of a party free of disability.

Nothing in this clause is to be construed as an assumption by the co-owners of the debts of a deceased or disabled owner for the purchase money obligation or expenses incurred but not paid at the time of the death or disability of a party; and no such obligation shall exist unless and only to the extent specifically stated elsewhere in this Agreement.

This clause requires the associates to approach the death or disability of an owner with charity. It may be regarded by many owners as too grand a gesture, but we think not. It's the kind of thing you are likely to want to do; at least, we found that to be true when we were confronted with the situation.

If one of the co-owners dies and the title passes to the other owners, as specified in the additional provision of the Ownership clause, all debts—at least those up to the value of the boat, and those incurred both before the death and afterward—are to be assumed by the surviving owners.

But if the additional provision is not used, and the deceased owner's interest goes into his estate, the surviving partners are to carry only those expenses occurring after the death, the estate of the deceased being liable for its share of the debts and expenses incurred before the time of death and those following the rejection of a sale.

The surviving owners may want to sell the boat or sell the deceased owner's interest. To provide a balance of power and discourage an estate representative from rejecting any offer deemed acceptable to the surviving owners, the estate may reject a sale, but only at the expense of picking up its *pro-rata* share of the fixed expenses incurred after the rejection.

The division of debt in case of the death of an owner can be handled another way if you wish. You could specify that the estate of the deceased continue to be responsible for its share of the fixed expenses (those that would be incurred if no use were made of the vessel), while the remaining owners take care of all the operating costs. But for the sake of the family of a deceased partner, it is often kinder to shift as much of the burden of ownership as you can to the surviving partners. Remember, our scheme provides an incentive to the owners to find a buyer for the deceased or disabled owner's interest, since they are stuck with all the expenses. If the estate has to pay fixed expenses, the remaining owners have less incentive to find a substitute.

This clause carries the unhappy merit of first-hand testing. During the writing of this book, one of our two partners suffered a fatal accident, lingering in a coma six months before he died. As written, the clause meets the legal exigencies of the situation while also fulfilling the emotional needs involved.

An emergency like this can be faced in any number of ways, to be sure. Our own course of action reflected a decision based on long, close friendships and our financial circumstances. But no matter how you decide to handle the economics of it in your own agreement, we do recommend that you make it clear that the surviving owners will immediately take upon themselves the ownership chores—that is, any boat-related paperwork or labor that had been the responsibility of the disabled or deceased owner.

In the absence of a definition of "permanent disability," it's doubtful that a court would adopt one to suit your purposes. The term should be relative to the context in which it is considered. A disability could mean anything from inability to perform some very specialized skill to inability to do any kind of work. A professional violinist who loses but a third of the little finger of his left hand has surely suffered a professional disability, but he could be at the helm of a boat the following weekend.

In this clause we define the term in the context of yachting.

Clearly, if an illness or incapacity is likely to endure beyond a full season, the situation is serious. The strain on the family budget is likely to be great; the chances of default increase with time; and few of us would want to take advantage of such a turn of events. For an association to have to limp along minus the benefits of a participating owner for more than that period of time would frustrate the purposes of the association; so the owners should be able to correct the situation. Unless, that is, the disabled owner wants to continue paying his share of the expenses in the interim.

Contrary to reason, people generally join an association for the first time with a certain amount of trepidation that mounts with the number of participants. But once the whole arrangement starts working, they realize how much of the enjoyment is lost if all the owners cannot be active and handy participants.

Decisions

29. In reaching our decisions, we will seek a true accord, with unanimity, predicated upon our stated objectives, good seamanship, and the fidelity of shipmates. However, in matters where this Agreement does not require unanimous consent, a majority vote shall be sufficient as long as the proposition is previously presented and discussed by all. Where there are but two participants, ties shall be broken by chance, if the parties agree, or by arbitration if they do not.

A delinquent party who is in default of this Agreement shall not be eligible to actually cast a vote, but shall be conclusively deemed to have cast it with the prevailing side.

The powers of those parties not in default shall include the power to amend in any particular the provisions of the following clauses: Insurance, Berth, Maintenance, Operations, Ship's Officers, Rules,

Ship's Log, Stowage, Third-Party Use, and Assessments.

In keeping with the casual nature of yachting, the agreement empowers you to make decisions without a formal meeting. The telephone is quite sufficient. However, the clause specifies that the majority cannot decide to do something without first giving the minority a chance to be heard.

You are better off to try for that "true accord"—a unanimous consent—in all decisions, even though no more than a majority consent is required for most of the decisions you will be making. First of all, it's better for the relationship if everyone comes around to one way of thinking. Also, you'll find that quite often the minority viewpoint contains merits not to be overlooked. While it may not alter your desire or determination to do something, the other opinion may in some way influence the way you do it—to everyone's advantage.

Arbitration

30. We shall resolve deadlocks deemed too important for determination by chance methods by submitting the matter to someone knowledgeable in yachting as our arbitrator. When we cannot agree on the selection of such a person, each party not in default will select a knowledgeable person, and those so selected, if they are an even number, may, if necessary, name one additional arbitrator who, with them, shall resolve the dispute through the application of the terms of this Agreement, including principles expressed in the Interpretation clause.

This clause does not deprive a party of the right to bring legal action to redress a wrong or to determine whether there has been a violation of the terms of the agreement. Nor does it provide a formal method of resolving disputes. But it does provide an intermediate course for resolving stubborn conflicts without incurring the legal expenses of a deadlock. The entire lot should be ashamed if they have to expose their inability to resolve their disputes to even one arbitrator. In the event they can't even agree on an arbitrator, it's probably time to see whether they can agree on a yacht broker.

If you want a more binding arbitration agreement than this clause provides, the attorney with whom you consult will undoubtedly have one available.

Forum of Jurisdiction

31. Should a co-owner ever be compelled to institute a lawsuit against any or all of the other co-owners pertaining in any way to this undertaking, such litigation may be instituted in the courts of the County of _____, Commonwealth/ State of _____. Or, if the claim is within its jurisdiction, then the claim may be brought in the U.S. District Court of the _____ District of _____.

    Each of us agrees to immediately submit to the injunctive powers of the court, accept service of process, and appear at the court in person or by counsel within the time prescribed by the court or within twenty days of the delivery of such process to us personally or to our last known address.

    Should one of us fail to submit to the court's jurisdiction and the court be unable to otherwise obtain jurisdiction over the defaulting party, the suit may be instituted in any other forum where jurisdiction can be acquired. In such case, the defaulting party shall pay all additional expenses (including, but not limited to counsel fees, transportation, meals, lodging, loss of earnings, and other expenses for the litigants and witnesses) resulting from the failure to submit to the jurisdiction of the designated court, plus any expenses and damages resulting from the party's failure

> or delay in complying with this provision. Such expenses are to be awarded regardless of the outcome of the litigation.

This provision anchors any lawsuits to the previously agreed-upon geographic area most convenient to the owners, regardless of how far from home the boat may be when the war of lawyers begins. It will either eliminate or mitigate the high costs of a suit in some distant court. Strategically, it reduces the leverage one owner might gain by filing suit in a remote court. Because of the mobility of yachts, this is always a possibility—but it's unlikely when he would be liable for the resulting expenses.

Again, don't let this talk of disputes and possible lawsuits scare you away from the benefits of jointly owning a boat. That would be like keeping your boat in port all year because of the statistical risk of fire, collision, or typhoon. Although you're much less likely to run into legal storms in the association than you are to have an occasional bout with heavy weather, it's wise to have this kind of contractual foul weather gear along with your oilskins. Then, if you do have a dispute, at least you won't be soaked with the added expense of travel and time lost from work.

If bad comes to worse, before embarking on an all-out forensic battle, you should point out to everyone involved one pertinent fact. That is, no judge can do any more for the parties than reasonable people can do for themselves—namely, to resolve the dispute. The parties should, in good faith, make every effort to do so before a judge enters the picture.

Before taking any matter to court, the owners would be well advised to sit down and give serious thought to what they could better do with the money they would spend on legal fees. And each one should be encouraged to reexamine his position by asking himself these questions: Is my position fair to everyone involved? What compromises am I willing to accept that will make it fair? As a final effort, the owners could ask themselves whether it doesn't make more sense to sell the boat than it does to embroil the association in endless dispute.

Additional Damages

32. In addition to other damages for which we may become responsible, a breach of this Agreement shall also make us liable for any loss or diminution in the use of the vessel occasioned by the breach, and for all expenses, including reasonable attorney fees, expended in an effort to obtain either performance or redress for the default.

Like the Forum of Jurisdiction clause, this provision should induce the partners to aim for compromise and compliance with the agreement rather than for the courtroom.

Perhaps no one would quarrel with the stipulation that a party in default pay for any loss of money or use of the boat that he causes. But you may wonder about the requirement that he also shell out for any legal fees incurred. This isn't for the purpose of making sure the legal profession gets paid, but to make sure an innocent party does not suffer a Pyrrhic victory, paying more to his lawyer than he recovers. For only one day in court, a good admiralty lawyer could cost you as much as an entire week of cruising—and a passel of them could set you back more than the value of the boat. For that reason alone, this Additional Damages clause serves an even more important function as a deterrent against a breach of the agreement and the use of the courts as a delaying tactic.

Punctuality

33. Because of the unforgiving nature of the sea and the necessity of diligence in our undertaking, the prompt and timely performance of this Agreement is mandatory, with time being of the essence in every respect of our Agreement.

The safety, preservation, conservation, and enjoyment of the boat, as well as your investment in it, depend in no small measure on the prompt performance of the duties created by the agreement.

The term "time is of the essence" is the legal way of bringing up the laggard and saying to everyone that prompt and timely performance is required. Any delay, no matter how slight, is a breach of the agreement and subjects the violator to the consequences of his default.

No Third-Party Rights

34. This Agreement shall not inure to the benefit of anyone except us, the owners, and our lawful representatives and permitted assigns; neither do we intend to create or vest any rights in third parties.

This clause makes sure that no one outside the association—creditors, boat mechanics, injured third parties, or the like—will be able to claim any rights other than those vested in them by law. Each provision of this contract is for the furtherance of the owners' welfare, and there should be no way in which any third party could lay claim to the benefits.

Executed this _____ day of _____,
19_____, in the ___ [City/County of] _____,
State of _____.

_____

_____

_____

7

Checklist

This chapter contains a checklist to use in a working session with your prospective partners. It lists the decisions you must make to complete your agreement and mentions some alternatives you may want to consider. When it's completed, you are ready for drafting, first as a do-it-yourself enterprise, preferably followed by legal assistance.

And in the process, you and your partners will have learned a lot about your boating preferences and about each other.

Checklist

The various clauses of the agreement, like those of any contract, must work together if your goal of a harmonious relationship is to be realized. Changing any part of the contract without first making sure that it doesn't conflict with any of the other parts could prove to be as disastrous as tinkering with the structure of your boat without consulting its designer. Your attorney will help ensure that your agreement fits together when he checks it over.

This checklist, when completed, will not only save time and effort in presenting your needs to the attorney; it also will streamline the mechanical work done by his staff in getting out the final copy—all of which, of course, saves you money.

As you and your prospective associates consider the decisions you will have to make for each clause and fill in the blanks for the specifications, you will need to draft any changes or alternative provisions separately, in your own words.

The possible alternatives are legion. In the clauses that deal with rules, berth location, and use schedules, you should consider the options most creatively, in light of your particular situation. Outside those areas, the agreement as printed is what we consider to be the most fair, consistent, and coherent approach to joint ownership for the majority of yachtsmen.

You will find the clauses in the checklist arranged in the same order as in the agreement, with spaces under each one for you to check off the various elements of the clause as you consider them, to note the specifications required by the agreement, and to indicate whether you prefer an alternative.

1. Purpose (page 31)

What are our primary purposes?
_____ long-term cruising
_____ short-term cruising
_____ racing
_____ fishing, shrimping, crabbing, etc.
_____ water skiing
_____ other: _____

Will these purposes require changes in other provisions of the agreement? _____

_____

(For instance, the manner of sharing the boat provided in

104

the Operations clause would be different from the contract as written here for racing with a crew or with the owners as crew, and for specialized fishing that occurs only at particular times of the year.)

_____ We want to change this clause according to Attachment #1.

2. Interpretation (page 32)

> The laws of the state of _____
> _____ shall govern this Agreement.

_____ We want to change this clause according to Attachment #2.

3. Adaptation (page 35)

Do we prefer to preclude oral amendments to the agreement?
_____ Yes   _____ No
(In most states, oral modifications of written agreements are recognized regardless of a provision in the original agreement precluding them. However, if you want to restrict the agreement to written amendments, you should bring this to the attention of counsel.)

_____ We want to change this clause according to Attachment #3.

4. Terms (page 37)

_____ We want to change this clause according to Attachment #4.

5. Ownership (page 38)

How shall we handle the title documents? Whose name or names will be on them? _____

Is the boat documented? _____

If not, do we want to apply for documentation? _____

In case of the death of one of us, do we want the title to pass to the surviving owner(s) by using the Additional Provision for Vesting Ownership in Survivors? _____

_____	type of boat
_____	year built
_____	name of builder
_____	name of boat
_____	state of registry
_____	name(s) on title
_____	purchase money creditor (if applicable)

_____ We want to change this clause according to Attachment #5.

6. Status of Association (page 40)

_____ We want to change this clause according to Attachment #6.

7. Lien Prohibition (page 41)

_____ We want to change this clause according to Attachment #7.

8. Insurance (page 42)

Do we need a marine survey to determine hull value? _____

What deductibles and limits do we want?

Type of risk	Deductible	Limit
_____	_____	_____
_____	_____	_____

---

full hull value
protection and indemnity limits
medical payments coverage per person
navigational limits
seasonal limits
value of trailer (if applicable)
liability limits for driver of towing vehicle (if applicable)

____ We want to change this clause according to attachment #8.

9. Uninsured Vessel Damages (page 46)

For damages due to simple negligence, do we want to limit a party's liability for uninsured portions to the deductible amount of the hull coverage, as the clause provides? _____

_____ We want to change this clause according to Attachment #9.

10. Uninsured Claims (page 52)

_____ We want to change this clause according to Attachment #10.

11. Unauthorized Use (page 56)

_____ We want to change this clause according to Attachment #11.

12. Notice of Insurance Cancellation (page 58)

_____ We want to change this clause according to Attachment #12.

13. Berth (page 60)

Will the area(s) chosen best serve our primary objectives (fishing, daysailing, cruising, racing, water skiing, etc.)?

_____

How convenient is the location for each of us in terms of travel time and traffic conditions during the peak boating season? _____

Does the location afford weather protection against high winds and water, or against the possibility of being iced in during winter if we plan to do any frostbiting?

_____

Is the water depth sufficient during low tide at the slip and along the routes away from the slip?

_____

Is it easily accessible from the water? Any adjacent bridges that would limit our hours of use?

_____

Does the marina or dock owner place any limitations on the maintenance work we want to do ourselves?

_____

Are the facilities adequate for our purposes? Do we prefer dockside availability of heads, showers, pumpout, trailer storage, repair operations, fuel, water, ice, food and drinks, restaurant, bar, parking, or recreational provisions?

_____

_____

Do we want a single or multiple berth?

_____

(Some alternatives to a single berth include splitting the

time between two designated berths; rotating the boat annually among several designated berths; or selecting a new berth annually if the majority desires).

Do we want to use the Option for Off-season Cruising in other waters? _____

_____ place(s) of berth	
_____ body of water	

_____ We want to change this clause according to Attachment #13.

14. Equipment (page 63)

The Equipment List, which is to be included in this Agreement, is set forth as Attachment #14-a.

Do we have any donated items of equipment? Are they gifts or loans? _____
_____

(Alternative to clause as written: designate the donated items "loaned by ___[name]___ " to the association under the conditions specified in the proviso that was suggested in the explanation of the clause.)

What equipment purchases are necessary to get the boat seaworthy and suitable for joint use? _____
_____

_____ We want to change this clause according to Attachment #14-b.

15. Maintenance (page 65)

What would be the estimated annual cost of yard maintenance? _____

Approximately how many man-hours would be required to maintain the boat ourselves? _____

_____

What preliminary work, if any, is to be done to get the boat seaworthy and acceptable for joint use? _____

_____

Which option of the agreement shall we use?
_____ Option A, for yard maintenance
_____ Option B, for owner maintenance, with individual choice of hiring someone to substitute

_____ We want to change this clause according to Attachment #15.

16. Utilization (page 70)

Will sharing the boat as written be compatible with our circumstances and our primary purposes

_____

(Some alternatives: daily assignment rotation for daysailers, runabouts, and other small craft; monthly (or longer) rotation for long-term cruising; assignments based on racing schedules, fish runs, employment, or school vacation schedules.)

> We want to restrict vacation scheduling to the months of _____
>
> _____

_____ We want to change this clause according to Attachment #16.

17. Ship's Officers (page 73)

How shall we determine the office of captain during the shakedown period? _____

_____

(Some alternatives to clause as written: rotation or selection of the most experienced owner on board).

How shall we handle the assignment of offices after the shakedown period? _____

_____

(Some alternatives to clause as written: assignment on a permanent basis or rotation of offices on request by a majority).

_____ We want to change this clause according to Attachment #17.

18. Operational Care (page 75)

_____ We want to change this clause according to Attachment #18.

19. Rules (page 76)

Suggestions for developing Rules:

Review the Rules in Appendix B.

Consider these areas: equipment operation; engine procedures; reporting of damage, malfunctions, and deficiencies; emergency procedures checklist; embarking and debarking procedures; guests.

Review operating instructions for engine and all equipment, and include the critical ones in the Rules.

Determine actual embarking procedures by going through them with a tape recorder.

Include in your emergency checklist the Coast Guard regulations for operating in hazard.

_____ We want to change this clause according to Attachment #19.

20. Ship's Log (page 77)

_____ We want to change this clause according to Attachment #20.

21. Stowage (page 78)

_____ We want to change this clause according to Attachment #21.

22. Third-Party Use (page 79)

_____ We want to change this clause according to Attachment #22.

23. Guests (page 81)

Do we want to place any restrictions on our right to invite guests aboard? _____

_____

(Some alternatives to clause as written: forbidding guests to serve as crew; limiting guests during particular types of boat use; for the sake of safety, precluding children under a certain age or the number of guests allowed at one time.)

_____ We want to change this clause according to Attachment #23.

24. Paid Crew (page 84)

_____ We want to change this clause according to Attachment #24.

25. Payment of Assessments (page 86)

> Rate of interest for any loans made by a co-owner to defaulting party: ____%

___ We want to change this clause according to Attachment #25.

26. Sale of Vessel (page 89)

_____ We want to change this clause according to Attachment #26.

27. Division of Proceeds (page 93)

_____ We want to change this clause according to Attachment #27.

28. Death or Disability (page 93)

_____ We want to change this clause according to Attachment #28.

29. Decisions (page 97)

_____ We want to change this clause according to Attachment #29.

30. Arbitration (page 98)

Do we want a more binding arbitration clause drawn up separately? _____

_____ We want to change this clause according to Attachment #30.

31. Forum of Jurisdiction (page 99)

_____ county of jurisdiction
_____ state of jurisdiction
_____ appropriate U.S. district court

_____ We want to change this clause according to Attachment #31.

32. Additional Damages (page 101)

_____ We want to change this clause according to Attachment #32.

33. Punctuality (page 101)

_____ We want to change this clause according to Attachment #33.

34. No Third-Party Rights (page 102)

_____ We want to change this clause according to Attachment #34.

Appendix

A

Notes to Counsel

This book contains too many caveats against its extraprofessional use to qualify as a "lay practice manual." Admittedly, the fact that it is written so that it may be distributed directly to clients does distinguish it from the many other practice aids found in any attorney's library. It is distinct also in that practical advice accompanies the document model. Though somewhat unusual, this approach permits a more efficient attorney-client relationship and results in substantial benefits to both.

For the client, there is the economy of time. Every document model, of course, saves the client the legal expense of countless hours that would otherwise be needed to accumulate the practical experience and legal knowledge for producing an original agreement. For example, a "scratch" draft of this agreement as an original undertaking would, of necessity, consume legal time of a value far in excess of the majority of boats sold in the United States today. However, this approach goes one step further. By furnishing the client a copy of the agreement, it also eliminates the generally convoluted process that takes place as the client, on one hand, conceptualizes his undertaking and considers the alternatives, while the attorney, on the other, determines the extent of accord, explains the agreement and its alternatives, and so on.

Of no little consequence to the profession is the rectification of a common misunderstanding between counsel and client regarding the use of practice aids. Within the profession, there is a solid appreciation of the advantages of using document models to deliver legal services. But far too often, a client who is not informed of their use and practicality at the outset makes the discovery long after the fact. Feeling cheated, the client never resumes the relationship, and the profession loses another opportunity to explain that the value of legal service lies in the selection of the proper model and its modification to comply with local laws and the particulars of the undertaking.

How an everyday occurrence so detrimental to both the individual practitioner and the profession is permitted to continue is difficult to explain. Undoubtedly, it is a holdover from earlier times when many clients were scarcely literate.

We wholeheartedly concur with those who warn against the indiscriminate distribution of practice aids. However, both the nature of this book and the demographic makeup of the yachting community provide general assurances that the book will be employed by people of above-average intelligence and wealth. Studies have shown the same profile for those who most often recognize and appreciate the value of legal services.

The risk that some among the yachting community may use the document without assistance of counsel is limited to those who are buying inexpensive boats or who would not seek legal counsel in any event. Disregarding all pride of authorship, it is fair to say that such people are nevertheless better off with this agreement as printed than with none at all.

The chance that the agreement will be misused must also

be assessed in light of the fact that people all over the country are entering into joint ownership relationships without the slightest benefit of either consultation or contract. Most attorneys practicing in areas near navigable waters are acquainted with people who own boats jointly; yet very few have ever been asked to furnish a contract of joint ownership. It is our sincere hope that this effort will go a long way toward correcting this potentially hazardous situation by emphasizing to the bar and the boating community the need for a joint ownership agreement, even among friends, and by providing for the first time in any volume known to us a document model that enables the bar to deliver the contract at a reasonable cost. The situation can only be improved.

The following reference notes should benefit the general practitioner who does not ordinarily handle admiralty cases or deal with the laws applicable to yachting. On the assumption that most attorneys called upon to furnish the agreement do not have access to an admiralty practitioner's library, source notes for the most part have been limited to the authorities available in most general practitioners' working libraries.

A cautious citator would almost invariably preface each citation with a customary *cf.*, for in many instances analogies must be drawn between cases involving yachting and those involving commercial vessels. Regrettably, many of the distinctions between the two have been ignored or overlooked by the courts.

There is yet another reason for a *cf.* State courts are not likely to apply many admiralty principles in nonadmiralty cases; but in determining issues of negligence, liability for collisions, and management rights in vessels, state courts would be well advised to look to the experience of admiralty courts.

A comprehensive survey of state statutes relating to boats is to be found in Benedict, *Admiralty* (7th ed.) Vol. 6A, pp. 843 *et seq.*

1. Purpose

• The fiducial relationship to which the clause refers arises in several ways.

a. The community of interest itself creates a relationship of mutual trust and confidence with regard to the jointly owned property. 20 Am.Jur. 2d, Cotenancy and Joint Ownership, § 2.

b. To the extent that the parties have authorized each other to act as agents, they of course assume a fiduciary relationship. 3 C.J.S., Agency, § 271.

c. Admiralty imposes upon the master (who, under this agreement, is the party using the vessel) a fiduciary duty to the owners. 70 Am.Jur. 2d, Shipping, § 164.

• The fiduciary relationship, however, does not preclude the parties from contracting with regard to the jointly owned property. 20 Am.Jur.2d, Contenancy and Joint Ownership, § 2.

2. Interpretation

• Much of what is in this clause and the preceding Purpose clause could be included in recital ("whereas") clauses. But as such, they would not be regarded as operative clauses. 17 Am.Jur.2d, Contracts, § 268; 17A C.J.S., Contracts, § 314. It was thought best to have them as operative clauses so they would have greater significance in controlling the application of the clauses entitled Rules, Decisions, and Arbitration.

• For a case which recognizes the right of the parties to select the laws of a particular forum with specific regard to vessels, see *Iberian Tanker Company* v. *Terminales Maracaibo, C.A.* 322 F.Supp. 73 (1971).

• Parties may select which law will govern their contract as long as the law selected has a reasonable relation to the transaction. 17 C.J.S., Contracts, § 12(3).

3. Adaptation

• Except for the few jurisdictions which by statute preclude oral modifications of contracts requiring written amendments, courts have been given to disregard such restrictions and permit oral modifications. 17 Am.Jur.2d, Contracts, § 467; 17A C.J.S., Contracts, § 377(C). Thus, the language of this clause is more likely to limit the effects of oral modifications than would a provision which purports to proscribe them.

• While confusion still exists as to the necessity of additional consideration for the modification of a contract, where the contract is executory and bilateral and where the original terms provide for modification, the original consideration should support modifications. 17 Am.Jur.2d, Contracts, § 469; 17A C.J.S., Contracts, § 376.

4. Terms

• For purposes of this agreement, the use of the words *yacht, vessel,* and *boat* as synonymous terms is of no consequence, but in the interpretation of various statutes, *motorboat, vessel, seagoing vessel,* etc., are distinguishing terms which require familiarity. Generally, for definitions and distinctions, see 12 Am.Jur.2d, Boats and Boating, § 1.

5. Ownership

• A yacht constitutes personal property, and its ownership is determined by the Common Law. 80 C.J.S., Shipping, § 13. For additional authority, see 70 Am.Jur.2d, Shipping, § 3.

• The registry of the vessel is not exclusive proof of its ownership. Thus, the written designation of one party as its owner and a contract that manifests other interests would be admissible to prove the interests of other owners. 80 C.J.S., Shipping, § 15.

• For a discussion of the effects of documentary recital on the validity of joint tenancy in community property states, see 15A Am.Jur.2d, Community Property, §§ 61, 62.

• Joint owners are presumed to have an equal interest. The presumption, however, is rebuttable, and other evidence is admissible to prove the parties' true interest. 80 C.J.S., Shipping, § 16.

• Admiralty recognizes as a matter of state law the co-ownership and partition of yachts. *Madruga* v. *Superior Court,* 346 U.S. 556, 74 S.Ct. 298, 98 L.Ed. 290.

• The relationship of co-owners is essentially the same as that of tenants in common of other chattels. 80 C.J.S., Shipping, § 16.

• The Federal Documentation Act does not preclude the registry of a vessel as joint tenants. Title 46 U.S.C.A., Chapter 2.

• While joint tenancies were originally confined to real property, tenancies of such character can now exist in any kind of property. 20 Am.Jur.2d, Cotenancy and Joint Ownership, § 6.

• The tendency of modern decisions is to place less emphasis on the formalistic requirements of the Common Law "four unities" and give greater emphasis to the intentions of the parties. 20 Am.Jur.2d, Cotenancy and Joint Ownership, § 4.

• Yachts are personal property and as such are subject to remedial process of attachment and execution. Their ownership and contracts related to them are admissible in courts of the Common Law, which also have jurisdiction over actions to recover possession. 70 Am.Jur.2d, Shipping, § 3.

• Most states, and certainly the federal government, require that the ship's documents be on board at all times during its operation. 70 Am.Jur.2d, Shipping, § 43.

• It should be remembered that a maritime lien is a secret one. 55 C.J.S., Maritime Liens, § 7. Such liens are not dependent upon possession. 55 C.J.S., Maritime Liens, § 5. Because they may operate to the prejudice of a purchaser without notice, it is imperative that precautions be taken against them when handling an acquisition.

• Generally, as to maritime liens against innocent purchasers, see 55 C.J.S., Maritime Liens, § 64(C).

6. Status of Association

• A cotenancy does not create an agency relationship between the owners. 20 Am.Jur.2d,

Contenancy and Joint Ownership, § 2. Thus, without specific authority, one cotenant cannot bind another. 20 Am.Jur.2d, Cotenancy and Joint Ownership, § 91.

• A captain, when confronted with an emergency or disaster, becomes an agent by necessity of the owners, insurers, and other parties at interest. He is granted the authority to do that which is necessary to save and protect the vessel from further harm. 70 Am.Jur.2d, Shipping, § 168.

• Unless the agency is coupled with an interest, the principal always has the power to terminate the agency relationship. However, the principal is answerable in damages for the violation of a contractual provision making the agency irrevocable. 2A C.J.S., Agency, § 112.

• Although an agency contract provides that an agency relationship is irrevocable, a principal may nevertheless revoke the same. However, he is answerable in damages for the violation of a contractual provision making the agency irrevocable. 2A C.J.S., Agency, § 112.

• Not only the death of the agent, but the death of a joint principal will terminate an agency relationship unless it is coupled with an interest or is separable. 2A C.J.S., Agency, § 139.

• However, an agency coupled with an interest is not revoked by either the insanity or the death of the principal. That is to say, the principal has neither the right nor the power to revoke the agency relationship absent the consent of the agent. 2A C.J.S., Agency, § 114.

• With regard to the power to contract for the survivorship of the agency following the mental incapacity of the principal, see 2A C.J.S., Agency, § 141.

7. Lien Prohibition

• As a general rule, one co-owner may not encumber jointly owned property, but even without the consent of the other owners he may encumber his own undivided interest. 20 Am.Jur.2d, Cotenancy and Joint Ownership, § 102.

• The captain of a vessel has the power to create a lien as security for payment of repairs and supplies in foreign ports. 70 Am.Jur.2d, Shipping, § 181.

• For a general discussion of the law pertaining to the incumbrances of jointly owned property, see 20 Am.Jur.2d, Cotenancy and Joint Ownership, Subdivision VII, § 93 *et seq.*

• For a general discussion of the law regarding liens, see Am.Jur.2d and 55 C.J.S., Maritime Liens.

• Precautions have been taken in this clause to prevent an interpretation which would treat any breach of the agreement as total and leave the injured parties with only an action in damages as their sole remedy. It is here specifically stated that the contract is to continue. The breach is to be treated as partial, as opposed to a total breach where remedial rights provided by law can be substituted by the injured party for only a part of the existing contractual rights. Restatement of the Law of Contracts, § 313.

8. Insurance

• For a most succinct discussion of marine insurance, see G. Gilmore and C. Black, *The Law of Admiralty* (2d ed. 1975), pp. 53–92.

• A more readily available discussion exists at 45 C.J.S., Insurance, §§ 852–876, 642–656.

• While a part-owner has no implied authority to insure the vessel, his acts may be ratified by the others, even after loss. 70 Am.Jur.2d, Shipping, § 250.

• A part-owner in control has been held liable for failure to insure his co-owner's interest in the vessel along with his own. 70 Am.Jur.2d, Shipping, § 262.

9. Uninsured Vessel Damages

• By general maritime law and the statutes of a number of states, the vessel itself (as well as perhaps the owners) is liable *in rem* for injuries or damages done through its willful or negligent operation. 70 Am.Jur.2d, Shipping, §§ 272–274.

• Absent an agreement, a captain/co-owner is held liable to part-owners for the value of their shares where the vessel is lost or damaged by his negligence. 70 Am.Jur.2d, Shipping, §§ 171, 262.

• For discussion and numerous authorities supporting the prerogative of parties to limit or preclude liability for simple negligence, see W. Prosser, *Law of Torts* (4th ed. 1971), Hornbook Series, p. 442.

10. Uninsured Claims

• For a general discussion of liability of yacht owners and operators for injuries and damages, see 12 Am.Jur.2d, Boats and Boating, Subdivision VII, §§ 32–68.

• For a collection of cases regarding liability of

an owner for injuries caused by another, see 71 A.L.R.3rd, 1018.

• Concerning liability of the owner or operator of a motorboat for injuries or damages, see 63 A.L.R.2d, 343.

• As to a general discussion of public policy regarding both indemnification and contribution, see W. Prosser, *Law of Torts* (4th ed. 1971), Hornbook Series, §§ 50, 51.

• Admiralty courts have not permitted contribution in noncollision cases. *Halcyon Lines* v. *Haenn Ship C. & R. Corp.,* 342 U.S. 282, 72 S.Ct. 277, 96 L.Ed. 318 (1952).

• Statutes exist in several states which would seem to preclude contribution among tort feasors and the application of comparative negligence in determining their respective liability. For a broadside condemnation of the "obvious lack of sense and justice" in these rules, see W. Prosser, *Law of Torts* (4th ed. 1971), Hornbook Series, p. 307.

• The clause which requires a party who causes the loss of insurance to indemnify the party who actually caused the mishap is subject to challenge on the grounds that it violates public policy. However, the duty to indemnify has been carefully limited to that which would have been provided under the insurance policy. Since such policies provide indemnification and are condoned, a forcible argument may be advanced for the validity of the provision.

• Though often criticized, the federal Limitation of Liabilities statute (46 U.S.C.A. 189) limiting the vicarious liability of vessel owners to the value of their respective interest in the vessel is applicable to yachts, regardless of their size. 63 A.L.R.2d, 364.

11. Unauthorized Use

• Of paramount concern to a co-owner is the use of the vessel by another co-owner when it is either uninsured or in a dangerous condition. For although part-owners of a vessel are not agents for each other (70 Am.Jur.2d, Shipping, § 249) and should not be held vicariously liable for the acts of a captain predicated upon a contractual relationship of master-owner (*Sturgis* v. *Boyer,* 24 How (U.S.) 110, 16 L.Ed. 591 (1860); *The Clarita and The Clara,* 23 Wall (U.S.) 1, 23 L.Ed. 146; 70 Am.Jur.2d, Shipping, § 350), nonetheless, a joint owner may be held liable for accidents caused by another, simply, for example, because of his consent to the use of the vessel (12 Am.Jur.2d, Boats and Boating, § 39) or for failure to provide a seaworthy vessel (12 Am.Jur.2d, Boats and Boating, § 33) or for his concurrent negligence (12 Am.Jur.2d, Boats and Boating, § 40). Also see 71 A.L.R.3rd, 1018.

• A most effective means of preventing the use of the vessel when it is in an unsafe condition is by reporting the matter to the Coast Guard, which has authority under 46 U.S.C.A. 1462 to terminate the use of the vessel and to order immediate steps to provide for its safety and for the safety of those on board.

• To assist the innocent owner, the clause stipulates a contractual conversion of the vessel for its use when it is uninsured. Following the conversion, the tort feasor, as owner *pro hac vice* (70 Am.Jur.2d, Shipping, §§ 243, 272) should be held liable for the torts of the vessel.

• While the general rule prevents an action in conversion by one cotenant against another, there are exceptions. 20 Am.Jur.2d, Cotenancy and Joint Ownership, §§ 85, 86. And in at least one case, the removal of property in violation of a contract of co-ownership has been held a conversion of the other co-owner's interest. *Grabes* v. *Fawcett* (Tex.Civ.App.) 307 S.W.2d 311 (1957).

• A part-owner who dissents to an intended voyage may obtain further exoneration by an open protest of the vessel's continued use (and in admiralty a demand for a stipulation for the vessel's safe return). 70 Am.Jur.2d, Shipping, §§ 247, 260; 80 C.J.S., Shipping, § 16(2).

12. Notice of Insurance Cancellation

• This provision must be sustained on general contract theories. If a similar provision has been employed, it apparently served its purpose well by avoiding litigation; for we have been unable to find a case interpreting a similar provision.

13. Berth

• A vessel at sea is regarded, in many ways, as if she were a part of the territory whose flag she flies; and as among the states, she is, at sea, regarded as a part of the state of her home port. 70 Am.Jur.2d, Shipping, § 7.

14. Equipment

• In addition to the criminal and civil sanctions against the use of a vessel without proper equipment, a violation of statutory requirements is negligence *per se,* 12 Am.Jur.2d, Boats and Boating, § 41.

• That is not to say that one is required to have on board only the equipment prescribed by statute. To meet admiralty's test of seaworthiness, the equipment required must be in good working order and commensurate to the waters and the task to which the vessel is put. See *The Southwark,* 191 U.S. 1, 8–9, 24 S.Ct. 1, 3, 48 L.Ed. 65 (1903); *Aguirre* v. *Citizens Casualty Co.,* 441 F.2d 141(5th Cir.1971).

• Simply having one life preserver on board for each person is insufficient to meet the requirements of 46 U.S.C.A. 526e. For it is also mandated that the preservers be "so placed as to be readily accessible."

• Not only must the required fire extinguishers be on board, they must be "kept in condition for immediate and effective use and shall be so placed as to be readily accessible." 46 U.S.C.A. 526g.

• Nor may one be assured in a criminal forum that a vessel equipped as required by statute will provide immunity to the owners. In the course of the prosecution of one Capt. LaBrecque for manslaughter under 18 U.S.C.A. 1112 for the loss of life due to negligence and inattention to duty under 18 U.S.C.A. 1115, and for the reckless operation of a vessel under 46 U.S.C.A. 1461(D), the court said, "Certainly the evidence concerning the absence of a radio is sufficient by itself to take the case to the jury on the issue of gross negligence." *United States* v. *LaBrecque,* 419 F.Supp. 430. There was neither a statute nor a regulation requiring the vessel, a yacht, to be equipped with a radio.

15. Maintenance

• In addition to liability founded on negligence, the owner of a vessel may be held liable for its unseaworthy condition. 70 Am.Jur.2d, Shipping, § 12. The doctrine imposes liability without fault and represents an absolute duty of the owner at all times to maintain the vessel in a reasonably fit condition under the circumstances. See notes to preceding Equipment clause.

• If, from neglect or bad faith, a vessel should leave port in an unseaworthy condition, an underwriter is likely to be held harmless from resulting losses. *N.Y., N.H. & H.R.R. Co.* v. *Gray,* 240 F.2d 460, 466, 1957 A.M.C. 616, 621 (2d Cir. 1957) certiorari denied 353 U.S. 966, 77 S.Ct. 1050 (1957).

• The Federal Ship Mortgage Act, which provides for lien rights to those furnishing repairs, supplies, and "other necessaries," is applicable to pleasure craft. 12 Am.Jur.2d, Boats and Boating, § 30.

• However, part-owners of vessels are not entitled to a maritime lien for advances superior to others having a maritime lien. *The Frank Brainerd,* 3 F.2d 664 (D.Me. 1925); *The Morning Star,* 1 F.2d 410 (W.D. Wash. 1924). And whether the owner advances the funds or takes an assignment, he shall fare no better insofar as his entitlement to a maritime lien. *The Congo,* 155 F.2d 492 (1946). But see notes to Payment of Assessments clause.

• For a discussion of the extent to which the Common Law recognizes liens between cotenants, see 20 Am.Jur.2d, Cotenancy and Joint Ownership, § 66.

• To the extent the lien is recognized under state law, it could be argued that it is subject to Article 9 of the Uniform Commercial Code that it must meet the filing requirements, and in the absence of filing it would be void against certain types of third-party creditors or purchasers. For a parallel argument in regard to admiralty claims, see G. Gilmore and C. Black, *The Law of Admiralty* (2d ed. 1975), p. 635.

• Where a party (principal) authorized another (agent) to hire a third party, the person employed becomes the employee of the principal, not of the agent. 3 Am.Jur.2d, Agency, § 7; Restatement of Agency 2d, § 5, Comment B.

• Considerable conflict exists as to a part-owner's authority to bind co-owners for repairs. 70 Am.Jur.2d, Shipping, § 270.

16. Utilization

• An analogy may be drawn from those cases which hold that it is in the interest of the owners (and perhaps the public) that a vessel be kept in trade. Likewise, a yacht should be kept at pleasure. Cf. 70 Am.Jur.2d, Shipping, § 257.

• During the break-in period when the vessel is being jointly used, it is doubtful that the part-owner who is then acting as captain is liable for injuries to or loss of the vessel, even if same is caused by his carelessness and negligence. 80 C.J.S., Shipping, § 16(4).

• Following the shakedown period, when the use of the vessel is exclusively vested in one of the owners, the relationship between them should be analogous to that of a vessel which is chartered "bareboat" for the interval of exclusive use. Under such circumstances, the operator of the vessel, the master, is regarded as the owner *pro hac vice,* and he alone is liable for the torts of the vessel. This is true even when commercial vessels are turned over to a master "on a lay," where the owners share in the profits of the voyage. For a general discussion of "letting on shares," see 70 Am.Jur.2d, Shipping, §§ 151 *et seq.* Also see *Williams* v. *Hays,* 38 N.E. 449 (N.Y. 1894).

17. Ship's Officers

• The master of the vessel is the person who has command of it. 70 Am.Jur.2d, Shipping, § 160. The power to appoint the master is, absent a contrary agreement, vested in the majority of co-owners. 70 Am.Jur.2d, Shipping, §§ 161, 258.

• Where one is authorized to order supplies by reason of their common interest, one part-owner has the implied power to bind the others for necessary supplies and repairs suitable and proper for the vessel. 80 C.J.S., Shipping, § 16(5).

• 46 C.F.R. 67.29–3 exempts yachts from the requirement that a change in master be reported to the officer in charge at the port where the change takes place. The regulations also permit the designation of two alternate masters. 46 C.F.R. 67.29–5.

• Those having one-half ownership may remove the master of a documented vessel, even if he is part-owner; but they may not do so if there is an agreement which entitles the master to possession. 46 U.S.C.A. 227.

• Under federal law, there is no requirement for a vessel of 15 tons or less to have a licensed crew, provided no passengers-for-hire are being transported. 46 U.S.C.A. 526f.

19. Rules

• Provisions regarding the power of a party to make rules binding upon another are commonly found in leases, where there is no mutuality of power, the landlord having the sole right to adopt such rules. His power, of course, is limited to the promulgation of reasonable rules. 49 Am.Jur.2d, Landlord & Tenant, § 246.

20. Ship's Log

• Counsel may wish to forewarn clients that while humor and jest spice up the ship's log, they have been admitted in evidence as official documents (50 A.L.R.2d, 1217) and as admissions against interest. 15 C.J.S., Collision, § 169.

22. Third-Party Use

• Absent an agreement, each part-owner would be entitled to a share of the chartering revenues proportionate to ownership. 70 Am.Jur.2d, Shipping, § 247.

• Even without an agreement, admiralty recognizes the power of a majority of part-owners to enter into a charter party agreement binding upon the minority. 80 C.J.S., Shipping, § 27.

• For a discussion of different types of maritime charter agreements, see *Williston on Contracts* (3rd ed.), § 1072–a.

• Counsel may want to limit the right or ability to charter to a "demise" or "bareboat" charter arrangement. We opted for providing the innocent parties greater alternatives.

• The demise charterer, as owner *pro hac vice*, assumes most, if not all, of the burdens of the actual owner. For a general discussion and further authority, see *Maysonet Gusman* v. *Pichirilo*, 369 U.S. 698, 8th L.Ed.2d 205, 82 S.C. 1095.

23. Guests

• For liability of the owner who temporarily relinquishes control of the vessel, see 71 A.L.R. 3rd, 1043. Although guests often serve as crew members, the owners' responsibilities toward them is not the same as those to be discussed in the next section pertaining to paid crew members.

• While it may not be negligence *per se* for a vessel to be under the control of a master who lacks the necessary license—15 C.J.S., Collision, § 10–11(1)—it does render the vessel unseaworthy, and for that reason the insurance policy may be voided.

• A license is required of any vessel transporting a passenger for hire. 46 U.S.C.A. 526f.

• "Every motor boat . . . while carrying passengers for hire, shall be operated or navigated by a person duly licensed for such service by the Coast Guard. . . ." 46 C.F.R. 157.30–30.

• Definition: "Carrying passengers for hire. The carriage of any person or persons by a vessel for a valuable consideration, whether directly or indirectly flowing to the owner, charterer, operator, agent or any other person interested in the vessel." 46 C.F.R. 24.10–3.

• Where one is required to have a license and does not, the vessel is unseaworthy. *Rowe* v.

Brooks, 329 F.2d, 35 (1964). As to an unseaworthy condition resulting in the suspension of
insurance coverage, see pertinent notes under
Maintenance clause.

• Social guests, though acting as members of a
crew, have been denied the preferred status of
"seaman." *Murphy* v. *Hutzel,* 27 F.Supp. 473
(1939).

• "The basis of the Kermarec decision is that
the vessel owner owes a duty of due care, not of
seaworthiness, to those aboard with the owner's
consent who are not in the privileged 'seaman'
class. In that case, it was also determined that
the Admiralty law would not differentiate between licensees and invitees." *Armour* v. *Gra-
dler,* 448 F.Supp. 741 (1978).

• The *Armour* case, *supra,* held that the doctrine of seaworthiness was inapplicable to two
friends fishing for recreational purposes. But see
In Re Read's Petition, 224 F.Supp. 241 (S.D.
Fla. 1963), where an unpaid member of a racing
crew was held to be a Jones Act seaman.

24. Paid Crew

• In admiralty, an agreement to pay wages to a
crew member gives the employee the preferred
status of seaman and imposes greater duties
upon the owners. Among other things, they are
responsible for providing maintenance and cure
benefits and are held to the absolute duty of
providing a seaworthy vessel. This duty has
nothing to do with negligence or fault. *Williston
on Contracts* (3rd ed.), § 1086–a.

25. Payment of Assessments

• For the right of a co-owner to a maritime lien for advancements, see notes under Maintenance clause.

• Where one co-owner makes expenditures for the repairs and supplies of a vessel, he is entitled to a lien. 80 C.J.S., Shipping, § 16.

• A part-owner who discharges a liability binding on all is entitled to contribution from the others in the proportions held by each. 70 Am.Jur.2d, Shipping, § 246.

• By Common Law, a part-owner is liable *in solido* for the whole amounts owed to third parties. However, in civil law states, it would appear that the part-owner's liability is proportioned to his "virile share" of the debt. 70 Am.Jur.2d, Shipping, § 254.

• Though part-owners have often been denied a maritime lien against co-owners, the question of entitlement is one of fairness to co-owners and other lienors. *The Puritan,* 258 Fed. 271 (1919).

• Generally, contracts do not terminate on breach. And where the parties have express provisions as to the effects of a breach, courts will give the breach only the effect stipulated. 17A C.J.S., Contracts, § 457.

26. Sale of Vessel

• A written bill of sale is required to transfer title to a documented vessel. 46 C.F.R. 67.45–3.

• For information concerning the administration of the estates of a deceased owner and the means of passing title to a documented vessel, see 46 C.F.R. 67.45–5.

• It should be remembered that a maritime lien is a secret one. 55 C.J.S., Maritime Liens, § 7. Such liens are not dependent upon possession. 55 C.J.S., Maritime Liens, §5. Because they may operate to the prejudice of a purchaser without notice, it is imperative that precautions be taken against them when handling a sale.

• Generally, as to maritime liens against innocent purchasers, see 55 C.J.S., Maritime Liens, § 64(C).

29. Decisions

• Even where there is no agreement, admiralty vests in the majority the control and management of a vessel. 70 Am.Jur.2d, Shipping, § 257.

30. Arbitration

• An arbitration clause does not *per se* bar an action for the enforcement of a contract. 6 C.J.S., Arbitration, § 28.

• Admiralty permits one who has agreed to arbitrate to nonetheless proceed with his liable for the seizure of a vessel. The parties may then be compelled to arbitrate. 9 U.S.C.A. 8.

31. Forum of Jurisdiction

• Where the yacht is employed in admiralty waters, courts of admiralty have jurisdiction over disputes between co-owners concerning the possession and use of the vessel. *Ward* v. *Thompson*, 22 How (U.S.) 330, 16 L.Ed. 249.

• Courts of equity may enjoin part-owners from the improper use, disposition, or destruction of the vessel. 70 Am.Jur.2d, Shipping, § 309.

• While a majority of jurisdictions do not regard a contractual agreement limiting causes of action to a particular court as a bar to litigation in other forums (56 A.L.R.2d, 306) such provisions may provide the right to a cause of action for damages arising from their breach. 56 A.L.R.2d, 311. Such clauses are also relevant to the issue of *forum non conveniens*. 90 A.L.R.2d, 1125.

• Before concluding from the specific discussion of maritime contracts in 56 A.L.R.2d, 316, that such contracts or provisions are invalid, see the 1972 decision of the Supreme Court of the United States in *Bremen* v. *Zapata Off-Shore Company,* 407 U.S. 1, 92 S.Ct. 1907, 32 L.Ed.2d, 513.

32. Additional Damages

• For conflicts of law questions concerning the enforceability of contractual provisions for attorney fees permitted by the state where the contract was executed or to be performed but not by the law of the forum, see 54 A.L.R.2d, 1053.

• The question of the extent to which provisions for attorney fees include payment for services rendered on appeal is discussed at 52 A.L.R.2d, 863.

33. Punctuality

• For a general discussion of the effects of specifying time to be of the essence, see *Williston on Contracts* (3rd ed.), §§ 845–856.

34. No Third-Party Rights

• For a discussion concerning the effects of the expression of the intent of the parties as to third-party beneficiaries, see *Williston on Contracts* (3rd ed.), § 356a, pp. 836–839.

Rules

Although you will undoubtedly have ideas for your own set of rules, these have particular significance for joint boating:

1. Licenses and ship's documents are to be stowed in _____[exact location]_____ and are not to be removed, except upon giving notice to the other owners.

Embarking

2. Inspection will be made of the vessel, rigging, safety equipment, stores, fuel and water tanks, oil reservoirs, and bilges.
3. Log entries will be read for any warnings.
4. Guests unfamiliar with this vessel will be shown the location of all safety equipment and instructed in the proper use of the head and any other equipment they will be using.

Debarking

5. The boat is to be left clean and neat:
   a. Open box of baking soda or pieces of charcoal will be left in icebox.
   b. No garbage or perishable foods will be left on board.
   c. Only those personal items of use to all will be left on board.
6. Log entry will be made, with engine time recorded and any warnings of damage or malfunction in bold print.
7. Additional warning of any disorder that would endanger or seriously inconvenience the next user will be made by placing a red warning tag on ignition.
8. Fuel and water tanks are to be topped off and oil reservoirs checked. If unable to replenish any of them, place a red warning tag on ignition with an explanation.
9. Vessel is to be returned at the appointed time. If user is unable to return to port by the end of his assigned time, he should make every effort to give notice of the delay.

Equipment: What and Where

An Equipment List for the jointly owned boat should include all items that are to be considered part of the boat's equipment and thus owned together. When the list is posted on board, absent-minded sailors have no excuse for stowing things in the wrong place. Even more important, you'll be able to find things in a hurry when you need them. The things that may be immediately required on deck in an emergency are kept in the most readily accessible stowage areas of the cockpit, secured for easy release. For more exacting owners wanting an annual review of the Rules, an equipment inventory will be a checklist for making any changes of stowage designation or methods of equipment use.

In developing a list tailored to your boat and your association, you will find Chapman's *Piloting, Seamanship and Small Boat Handling* most helpful. (You might begin by making the book a part of your equipment.) Chapman's divides a boat's equipment into three easily defined categories. First are the items that are legally required: lifesaving equipment, personal flotation devices, fire extinguisher, and the like. Next is the additional safety equipment you may want on board: extra fire extinguishers, a spare anchor, distress signaling equipment, whistles for you and your guests to wear around the neck and help locate anyone who falls overboard. The last group includes those things you want for your convenience and comfort. In time, this is bound to become the fattest part of your list.

After deciding what you are going to need in the way of equipment, or which items to designate jointly owned among the items the boat already carries, you may be wondering where you should stow it to everyone's advantage. This doesn't take long to determine if you apply two simple principles: accessibility and protection from the elements. You wouldn't, for instance, put the flashlight batteries in an exposed cockpit bin and stash the life vests below. *Would* you?

By making a Supplies Reminder List, a sample of which follows the Equipment List, you can more easily keep up with all those little things that yachtsmen invariably discover are gone just when they most need them. (*"What, no charcoal? And we just paid a pirate's ransom for these steaks!"*) Nothing so challenges one's ingenuity as running out of garbage bags or paper towels when the nearest marina store is two days away.

The bosun should periodically check supplies and report to the purser any items that are running low. In the meantime, those who use the boat are responsible for reporting to the purser anything they notice that needs to be replenished.

Your basic list of safety items will be similar to the inventories of other boats of your type and size. Beyond that, however, your equipment collection is bound to differ according to your navigational area, the type of yachting you do, and your individual tastes. We personally wouldn't expect everyone else who owns a sailing sloop (or anyone else, for that matter) to prefer a conch shell over a pressurized foghorn; or to fancy keeping water hot all day in a Chinese thermos rather than lighting the swing stove whenever someone wants coffee or instant soup. Those, of course, are our most practical eccentricities: we decline to reveal the others.

The following sample Equipment List cannot reflect in detail the needs of every yacht and ownership group. It excludes special gear for racing, water skiing, fishing, snorkeling, or scuba diving. And some of the optionals that are listed won't be found on all boats—the Loran, the radio-telephone, the sextant, and related celestial navigation supplies, to name a few. Otherwise, it's fairly representative of well-equipped motor and sailing yachts in the thirty- to sixty-foot range.

We would warn any novice yachtsmen using this list that the requirements for safety equipment are constantly changing. Even if you don't intend to have an annual review of the Rules, a yearly stock-taking of the safety equipment by the bosun can ensure that your collection stays in conformance with the latest Coast Guard regulations.

You may prefer to develop your own list of equipment in an entirely different way. That doesn't matter. The important thing is that you at least decide what's yours, what's mine, and what's ours, and that you keep a list of it handy for everyone.

Equipment List

Cockpit and Deck

Readily Accessible (specify which locker):

Anchor light	Compass
Bailing scoop	Dinghy (oars, oarlocks, bailing
Binoculars	scoop, painter inside)
Boarding ladder	Dinghy motor and fuel tank
Boathook	Distress signal kit (if it can be
Buoyant ring and line	kept dry here)
Buoyant cushions	Dock lines

143

Fire extinguisher
Flashlight (heavy duty)
Fog bell
Horn
Inflatable raft, and lashed to it in a waterproof bag: instructions for use, oars, drinking water, knife, bailer, sponge, flares, seasick pills, small first-aid kit, candy)
Knife with marlinspike (sailboats only)
Life vests
Man overboard marker
Safety harness (sailboats only)

Sheath knife
Vise grips
Sheets (sailboats only)
Spare anchor, line, and chain
Winch handles (sailboats only)

Remote Storage Areas:

Bucket (plastic) and attached line
Charcoal grill
Ensigns
Fenders
Fuel can
Maintenance gear (deck brush, mop, sponges, rags)

Cabin

Navigation area:

Binoculars
Chapman's and other manuals
Charts
Chronometer
Compass
Cruising guides
Dividers
Hand-bearing compass
Log
Nautical almanac
Paper (large notepads)
Parallel rulers
Pens and pencils
Radiotelephone
Sextant
Sight reduction tables
Star finder
Tide tables
Weather radio

Clock
Depth finder
Fire extinguisher(s)
Inclinometer
Marine radio

Chain Locker:

Anchor rode and chain

Engine Area:

Batteries and charger
Electrical tape
Engine manual
Flashlight
Fuses
Spare engine parts
Spare bulbs
Tool kit

Bulkheads:

Aluminum mirror
Barometer

Forward Storage Bins:

All sails and related equipment
Sea anchor

Appendix C

Cabin Lockers:

Alarm clock
Bilge pump
Blanket (for emergency use)
Cabin heater
Clothes hangers (plastic or wood)
First-aid kit (including sunscreen
    and motion sickness pills)
Hatch screens
Radar reflector
Transistor radio
Water jugs (collapsible)
Miscellaneous (ashtrays, playing
    cards, sewing kit, extra
    sunglasses, spare foul weather
    gear)

Coffee pot
Coffee mugs
Dish towels
Flatwear
Glasses (plastic)
Granny fork
Icepick
Knives (butcher, paring, steak)
Mixing bowls
Plates (plastic)
Potholders
Pots, pans, skillets
Spatulas
Whisk
Swing stove and parts
Thermos
Pressure cooker

Galley Lockers:

Bottle openers/corkscrew
Can opener

Supplies Reminder List

Alcohol for stove
Batteries
Charcoal and lighter fluid
Engine oil
Fiberglass cleaner
First-aid supplies
Fuel (spare)
Fuses
Garbage bags
Glass cleaner
Head supplies: toothpaste, hand
    lotion, soap, shaving cream,
    tissues, toilet paper

Household cleaner
Insect repellent
Lamp oil
Liquid dish detergent
Matches
Paper, pens, pencils
Paper towels
Scrub buds
Spices and herbs
Sugar, salt, pepper
Sponges
Sterno cartridges
Teak polish

145

INDEX

Index